The Best Songs Ever

T0081582

ISBN 978-1-4803-3024-5

HAL•LEONARD®
CORPORATION

7777 W. BLUEMOUND RD. P.O. BOX 13819 MILWAUKEE, WI 53213

Visit Hal Leonard Online at
www.halleonard.com

Contents

All I Ask of You

from THE PHANTOM OF THE OPERA

Music by Andrew Lloyd Webber
Lyrics by Charles Hart
Additional Lyrics by Richard Stilgoe

Melody:

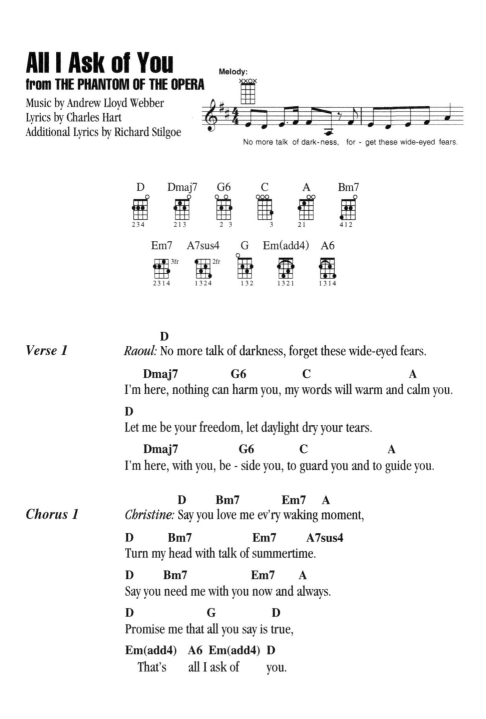

No more talk of dark-ness, for - get these wide-eyed fears.

Verse 1

> **D**
> *Raoul:* No more talk of darkness, forget these wide-eyed fears.
>
> **Dmaj7**   **G6**   **C**   **A**
> I'm here, nothing can harm you, my words will warm and calm you.
>
> **D**
> Let me be your freedom, let daylight dry your tears.
>
> **Dmaj7**   **G6**   **C**   **A**
> I'm here, with you, be - side you, to guard you and to guide you.

Chorus 1

> **D**   **Bm7**   **Em7**   **A**
> *Christine:* Say you love me ev'ry waking moment,
>
> **D**   **Bm7**   **Em7**   **A7sus4**
> Turn my head with talk of summertime.
>
> **D**   **Bm7**   **Em7**   **A**
> Say you need me with you now and always.
>
> **D**   **G**   **D**
> Promise me that all you say is true,
>
> **Em(add4)**   **A6**   **Em(add4)**   **D**
> That's   all I ask of   you.

Verse 2

          D
Raoul: Let me be your shelter, let me be your light.

    Dmaj7   **G6**   **C**   **A**
You're safe, no one will find you, your fears are far be - hind you.

     D
Christine: All I want is freedom, a world with no more night.

  Dmaj7   **G6**   **C**   **A**
And you, always be - side me, to hold me and to hide me.

Chorus 2

       D   **Bm7**   **Em7** **A**
Raoul: Then say you'll share with me one love, one lifetime

D **Bm7**   **Em7**   **A**
Let me lead you from your solitude.

D **Bm7**   **Em7**   **A**
Say you need me with you, here be - side you.

D   **G**   **D**
Anywhere you go, let me go too.

A7sus4   **A6** **A7sus4 D**
Christine, that's all I ask of   you.

Chorus 3

       D   **Bm7**   **Em7** **A**
Christine: Say you'll share with me one love, one lifetime.

D **Bm7**   **Em7**   **A7sus4**
Say the word and I will follow you.

D   **Bm7**   **Em7**   **A**
Share each day with me, each night, each morning.

D   **G**   **D**
Say you love me. *Raoul:* You know I do.

         A7sus4   **A6** **A7sus4 D**
Christine & Raoul: Love me, that's all I ask of   you.

Interlude |**D**   **Bm7** |**Em7** **A** |**D**   **Bm7** |
               |**Em7** **A7sus4** |**D**   **Bm7** |**Em7** **A** |

Outro

                  D   **G**   **D**
Christine & Raoul: Anywhere you go, let me go too.

A7sus4   **A6** **A7sus4 D**
Love me, that's all I ask of   you.

All the Things You Are
from VERY WARM FOR MAY

Lyrics by Oscar Hammerstein II
Music by Jerome Kern

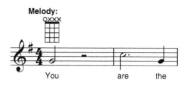

Melody:

You   are   the

Em7   Am7   D7   Gmaj7   Cmaj7   F#7   Bmaj7   Bm7

A7   Dmaj7   G#7b5   C#7   F#maj7   D#7#9   G#m7   Fm7b5

Bb7   Ebmaj7   B7#5   F13   A#°7   F#m7b5   B7b9

Verse 1

Em7 Am7   D7   Gmaj7
You   are the promised kiss of springtime
Cmaj7   F#7   Bmaj7
That makes the lovely winter seem long.

Bm7 Em7   A7   Dmaj7
You   are the breathless hush of evening
Gmaj7   G#m7b5 C#7 F#maj7
That trembles on the brink of a lovely song.

Bridge

D#7#9 G#m7   C#7   F#maj7
You are the angel glow   that lights a star.
Fm7b5   Bb7   Ebmaj7 B7#5
The dearest things I know   are what you are.

Verse 2

Em7   Am7   D7   Gmaj7
Some - day my happy arms will hold you,
Cmaj7 F13   Bm7   A#°7
And some - day I'll know that moment di - vine,
Am7   D7   Gmaj7 (F#m7b5) (B7b9)
When all the things you are are mine.

Always

Words and Music by
Irving Berlin

Melody:

Ev - 'ry-thing went wrong,

Bb6	Gm7b5	F	G7	C7	F#°7	Gm7
3241	111	2 1	213	1	1324	211

F7	Am	E7	A	Eb7	D7	Gm
2314	2	12 3	21	1112	2 3	231

Intro
| Bb6 | Gm7b5 | F | G7 | |
| C7 | | F | | |

Verse 1

F   F#°7
Ev'rything went wrong,

C7
And the whole day long

  Gm7 C7   F
I'd feel _____ so blue.

           F#°7
For the longest while

C7
I'd forget to smile.

   Gm7 C7   F F7
Then I _____ met you.

Am   F7   E7
Now that my blue days have passed,

           Am F#°7 C7
Now that I've found you at last,

Chorus 1

F
I'll be loving you, always

C7   F
With a love that's true, always.

                        F7
When the things you've planned

A
Need a helping hand,

E7   A   C7
I will understand, always, always.

F   F7   E7 E♭7
Days may not be fair, always.

D7   Gm
That's when I'll be there, always,

B♭6   Gm7♭5 F   G7
Not just for an hour,   not just for a day,

C7   F   C7
Not just for a year, but always.

Verse 2

F   F#°7
Dreams will all come true,

C7
Growing old with you,

Gm7 C7   F
And time ____ will fly,

                  F#°7
Caring each day more

C7
Than the day before,

Gm7   C7   F F7
'Till spring ____ rolls by.

Am   F7   E7
Then when the springtime has gone,

             Am F#°7 C7
Then will my love linger on.

Chorus 2

F
I'll be loving you, always

C7   **F**
With a love that's true, always.

                    F7
When the things you've planned

A
Need a helping hand,

E7   **A**   **C7**
I will understand, always, always.

F   **F7**   **E7** **E♭7**
Days may not be fair, always.

D7   **Gm**
That's when I'll be there, always,

B♭6   **Gm7♭5** **F**   **G7**
Not just for an hour,   not just for a day,

C7   **F**
Not just for a year, but always.

Almost Like Being in Love

from BRIGADOON

Lyrics by Alan Jay Lerner
Music by Frederick Loewe

Melody:

May - be the sun   gave me the pow'r,

F7 F°7 C#°7 F Cm7 Dm Bb7 Fm7 Ebmaj7

Bbmaj7 F+ Bb6 Eb Bb Gm Bb7#5 Am7 D7sus4

D+ G Am7b5 D7 Eb7 Gb7 Em7b5

Intro

| F7   F°7 | F7   C#°7 |

Verse

F Cm7 Dm   Cm7
Maybe the sun gave me the pow'r,

F7   Cm7
But I could swim Loch Lomond

F7   Cm7
And be home in half an hour.

Bb7 Fm7 Bb7   Fm7
Maybe the air gave me the drive

Bb7 Fm7   Bb7
For I'm all a - glow and a - live.

Chorus

Ebmaj7   Cm7   F7
What a day   this has been!

Bbmaj7   F+   Bb6
What a rare mood I'm in!

Cm7   Eb   F7 Bb
Why, it's   almost like being in   love.

Gm   Bb7#5 Ebmaj7 Cm7 F7
There's a   smile   on my face

Bbmaj7   F+   Bb6
For the whole hu - man race.

Cm7   Eb   F7 Bb
Why, it's   almost like being in   love!

Bridge

Am7   F°7   D7sus4
All the music of   life

D+   G
Seems to be

Eb   Am7b5   D7
Like a bell that is ringing for me.

Outro

D+ D7   F°7
And from the

Ebmaj7 Cm7 F7
Way   that I feel

Bbmaj7   F+   Bb6
When that bell starts to   peal

Cm7   Eb7
I would swear I was falling,

Bb   Gm
I could swear I was falling.

Gb7 Bb Em7b5   F7   Bb
It's   al - most like being in love.

At Last

Lyric by Mack Gordon
Music by Harry Warren

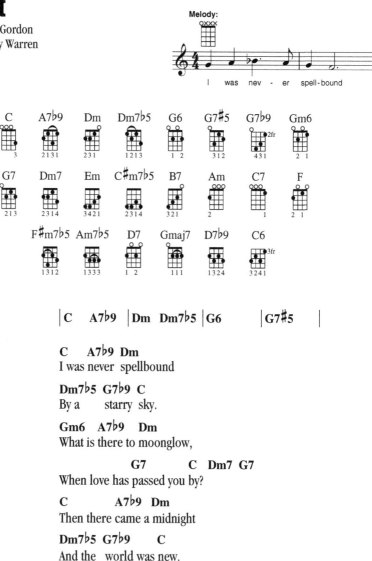

Melody:

I was nev - er spell-bound

Intro

| C A7♭9 | Dm Dm7♭5 | G6 | G7♯5 |

Prelude

C   A7♭9 Dm
I was never spellbound

Dm7♭5 G7♭9 C
By a   starry sky.

Gm6   A7♭9   Dm
What is there to moonglow,

              G7   C Dm7 G7
When love has passed you by?

C   A7♭9 Dm
Then there came a midnight

Dm7♭5 G7♭9   C
And the   world was new.

       Em   C♯m7♭5   B7
Now here I am so spellbound, darling,

    Em C♯m7♭5 Dm7 G7♯5
Not by stars, but just by you.

Verse

   C   Am Dm7   G7   C Am
At last _____ my love ___ has come along,

Dm7   G7   C Am
My lone - ly days are over

Dm7   Dm7♭5 G7   C Am Dm7♭5
And life ___ is like a song.

G7♯5 G7 C Am Dm7   G7   C   Am
At last _____ the skies ___ above are blue,

Dm7   G7♯5   G7   C   Am
My heart ___ was wrapped in clover

Dm7   Dm7♭5 G7   C   Dm7♭5 G7 C
The night ___ I looked at you.

Bridge

C7   F
I found a dream

 G7♭9 C
That I can speak to.

        F♯m7♭5 B7   Em
A dream that I can   call my own.

        Am7♭5 D7   Gmaj7
I found a thrill to press my cheek to,

 Am   D7♭9   G7 G7♯5
A thrill I've never known.

Outro

    C   Am Dm7   G7   C Am
You smiled _____ and then ___ the spell was cast

Dm7   G7♯5   G7   C   Am
And here ___ we are in heaven

Dm7   G7   C Dm7♭5 G7 C6
For you are mine at last.

Bewitched

from PAL JOEY
Words by Lorenz Hart
Music by Richard Rodgers

Melody:

I'm wild a-gain, be - guiled a-gain,

Cmaj7 C#°7 Dm7 D#°7 C E7 Fmaj7 F#°7

G7 A7♭9 Gm7 C7 Em7♭5 Dm Dm(maj7) Dm6

Am Am(maj7) Am7 Am6 Em7 C6

Verse 1

>   Cmaj7   C#°7   Dm7   D#°7
> I'm wild again, ___ be - guiled again,
>
>   C   E7   Fmaj7
> A simpering, whimpering child again.
>
> F#°7   C   D#°7
> Be - witched, bothered
>
>   Dm7   G7 A7♭9 Dm7 G7
> And be - wildered ___ am   I.

Verse 2

>   Cmaj7   C#°7   Dm7   D#°7
> Couldn't sleep, ___ and wouldn't sleep,
>
>   C   E7   Fmaj7
> When love came and told me I shouldn't sleep.
>
> F#°7   C   D#°7
> Be - witched, bothered
>
>   Dm7   Gm7 C7 Fmaj7 Em7♭5 A7♭9
> And be - wildered ___ am   I.

Bridge

Dm   Dm(maj7)   Dm7 Dm6

Lost my heart, ____ but what of it?

Am   Am(maj7) Am7 Am6

He is cold, ____ I a - gree,

Dm7   G7   Dm7 G7

He can laugh, ____ but I love it,

Em7   D#°7 Dm7

Although the laugh's on   me.

Verse 3

G7 Cmaj7   C#°7   Dm7   D#°7

I'll sing to him, ____ each spring to him,

C   E7   Fmaj7

And long for the day when I'll cling to him.

F#°7 C   D#°7

Be - witched, bothered

Dm7   G7   C6

And be - wildered ____ am I.

Blue Skies
from BETSY
Words and Music by
Irving Berlin

Melody:

I was blue, just as blue as I could

G G7 C6 C7 G6 Gm6 A7

Bm F#+ F#7 D7 B+ Em B7

C#m7b5 Cm6 C9 D+ F#m7b5 B7#5 Cm

Verse 1

   G   G7   C6   C7   G
I was blue, just as blue as I could be.

   G7   C6   G6 Gm6 A7
Ev'ry day was a cloudy day for   me.

Bm   F#+   F#7   D7
Then good luck came a - knocking at my door.

G   G7   C6   C7 G   B+
Skies were gray but they're not gray any - more.

Chorus 1

   Em   B+ B7   G
Blue skies ___ smiling at me.

C#m7b5 D7   Cm6 G   C9 D+   G F#m7b5 B7#5
Nothing but   blue skies ___ do I see.

   Em   B+ B7   G
Bluebirds ___ singing a song,

C#m7b5 D7   Cm6 G   C9 D+   G
Nothing but   bluebirds ___ all day long.

Bridge 1

```
G              Cm      G
Never saw the sun shining so bright.

Cm     G   Cm     G
Never saw things going so right.

            Cm      G
Noticing the days hurrying by,

Cm          G    F#m7b5      B7#5
When you're in love, my, how they fly.
```

Chorus 2

```
Em      B+  B7#5      G
Blue days, ___ all of them gone.

C#m7b5  D7    Cm6 G        C9 D+      G
Nothing but    blue skies ___ from now on.
```

Verse 2

```
G     G7    C6       C7    G
I should care if the wind blows east or west.

        G7     C6         G6 Gm6 A7
I should fret if the worst looks like the    best.

Bm      F#+       F#7          D7
I should mind if they say it can't be true.

G     G7              C6  C7   G B+
I should smile if that's ex - actly what I do.
```

Chorus 3   *Repeat Chorus 1*

Bridge 2   *Repeat Bridge 1*

Outro   *Repeat Chorus 2*

Body and Soul

Words by Edward Heyman,
Robert Sour and Frank Eyton
Music by John Green

Melody:

My heart is sad and lone - ly,

Fm7　C7b9　Bb7　Ebmaj7　Ab7　Gm7　F#°7　Dm7b5　G7

Cm7　Eb6　F#m7　B7　Emaj7　E　Am7　D7　G#m7

C#m7　Em7　A7　Dmaj7　F°7　Db7　C7

Verse 1

> **Fm7　　　C7b9　Fm7　Bb7**
> My heart is sad and lonely,
>
> **Ebmaj7　Ab7　Gm7　　F#°7**
> For you I sigh, for you, dear, only.
>
> **Fm7　　　　Dm7b5　G7**
> Why haven't you seen　　it?
>
> **Cm7　　Fm7　Bb7　　　Eb6　C7b9**
> I'm all for you,　body and soul!

Verse 2

> **Fm7　　　C7b9　Fm7　Bb7**
> I spend my days in longing
>
> **Ebmaj7　　　Ab7　Gm7　　F#°7**
> And wond'ring why it's me you're wronging.
>
> **Fm7　　　Dm7b5　G7**
> I tell you I mean　　it
>
> **Cm7　　Fm7　Bb7　　　Eb6　F#m7　B7**
> I'm all for you,　body and soul

Bridge

Emaj7   F#m7   E   Am7 D7
I can't be - lieve it, it's hard to con - ceive ___ it

G#m7   C#m7 F#m7 B7 Emaj7
That you'd turn ___ a - way   ro - mance.

Em7   A7   Dmaj7   F°7
Are you pre - tending, it looks like the ending

Em7   A7   D7   Db7 C7
Un - less I could have one more chance to   prove, dear?

Verse 3

Fm7   C7b9   Fm7 Bb7
My life a wreck you're making,

Ebmaj7   Ab7   Gm7 F#°7
You know I'm yours for just the taking.

Fm7   Dm7b5 G7
I'll gladly sur - ren - der

Cm7   Fm7 Bb7   Eb6
Myself to you,   body and soul!

Call Me Irresponsible

from the Paramount Picture

PAPA'S DELICATE CONDITION

Words by Sammy Cahn
Music by James Van Heusen

Melody:

Call me ir - re-spon - si - ble,

F   F6   Gm   C7   F#°7   Gm6   G#°7   Am   A7

D7#5   Am7b5   D+   D7   G7   Gm7   C7#5   D7b9   C7b9

Intro

‖: F   F6 |Gm   C7   :‖

Verse 1

F   F6   F#°7
Call me irresponsible,

Gm   Gm6   G#°7
Call me   unreliable,

Am   F   A7   D7#5   Am   Am7b5   D7#5
Throw in undependable, too.

Gm   F#°7   C7   Am7b5   F#°7   D+   D7
Do my fool - ish alibis bore   you?

F6   G7
Well, I'm not too clever.

Gm7   C7   C7#5
I just adore you.

Verse 2

F   F6   F♯°7
Call me unpredictable,

Gm Gm6 G♯°7
Tell me   I'm impractical,

Am   F   A7   D7
Rain - bows I'm inclined to pur - sue.

Gm   F♯°7 C7
Call me ir - responsible,

Am7♭5 D7
Yes, I'm unreliable,

Gm   F♯°7 C7   A7 D7♭9
But it's un - deniably true,

D7 Gm   C7♭9   F
I'm irresponsibly mad for you!

Can't Help Falling in Love

from the Paramount Picture BLUE HAWAII

Words and Music by George David Weiss,
Hugo Peretti and Luigi Creatore

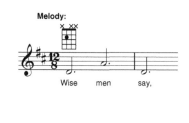

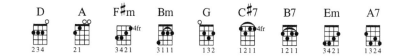

Intro

|D A |D |

Verse 1

D F#m Bm   G   D   A
Wise men say, only fools rush in.

G A   Bm G   D A D
But I can't help falling in love with you.

Verse 2

D   F#m Bm
Shall I   stay?

G D A
Would it be a sin

G A Bm G   D A D
If I can't help falling in love with you?

Bridge 1

F#m   C#7 F#m   C#7
Like a river flows surely to the sea,

F#m   C#7
Darling, so it goes.

F#m   B7   Em A7
Some things   are meant to be.

Verse 3

D F#m Bm   G   D   A
Take my   hand, take my whole life, too.

  G A   Bm G   D   A   D
For I can't help falling in love with you.

Bridge 2

Repeat Bridge 1

Verse 4

D F#m Bm   G   D   A
Take my   hand, take my whole life, too.

  G A   Bm G   D   A   D
For I can't help falling in love with you.

  G A   Bm G   D   A   D
For I can't help falling in love with you.

Candle in the Wind

Words and Music by
Elton John and Bernie Taupin

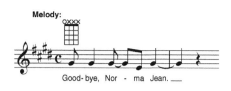

Melody:

Good-bye, Nor - ma Jean. ___

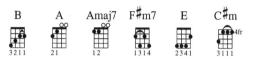

B   A   Amaj7   F#m7   E   C#m

Intro　　|B　　　　|A　Amaj7　F#m7 |E　　　|B　　　　　|

Verse 1
>   E   A
> Goodbye, Norma Jean. Though I never   knew you at all
>
>   E   A
> You had the grace to hold yourself while those around you crawled.
>
>   E   A
> They crawled out of the woodwork and they whispered   into your brain.
>
>   E   A
> They set you on the tread - mill and they made you change your name.

Chorus 1
>   B   E   A
> And it seems to me you lived your life like a candle in the wind,
>
>   E   B
> Never knowing who to cling to when the rain __ set in.
>
>   A   C#m
> And I would __ have liked to have known you, but I was just ___ a kid.
>
>   B   A
> Your candle burned out long before your legend ever did.

Interlude 1　　|A　Amaj7　F#m7 |E　　　|　　　　|B　　　|
　　　　　　　　|A　Amaj7　F#m7 |E　　|B　　|　|

Verse 2

```
         E                              A
Loneliness was tough, the toughest role   you ever played.
                          E                                A
Hollywood created a su - perstar and pain was the price you paid.
                  E              A
Even when you died, oh, the press __ still hounded you.
                       E                           A
All the papers had __ to say was that Marilyn was found in the nude.
```

Chorus 2   *Repeat Chorus 1*

Interlude 2   *Repeat Interlude 1*

Verse 3

```
         E                              A
Goodbye, Norma Jean. Though I never   knew you at all
                            E                              A
You had the grace to hold __ yourself while those around you crawled.
E                                          A
Goodbye, Norma Jean, from the young man in the twenty-second row
                               E
Who sees you as something more __ than sexual,
                       A
More than just our Marilyn __ Monroe.
```

Chorus 3

```
            B                         E           A
And it seems to me you lived your life like a candle in the wind,
            E                               B
Never knowing who to cling to when the rain __ set in.
            A                                   C#m
And I would __ have liked to have known you, but I was just ___ a kid.
                  B               A           Amaj7  F#m7  E
Your candle burned out long before your legend ever did.
                  B               A           Amaj7  F#m7  E
Your candle burned out long before your legend ever did.
```

Climb Ev'ry Mountain

from THE SOUND OF MUSIC

Lyrics by Oscar Hammerstein II
Music by Richard Rodgers

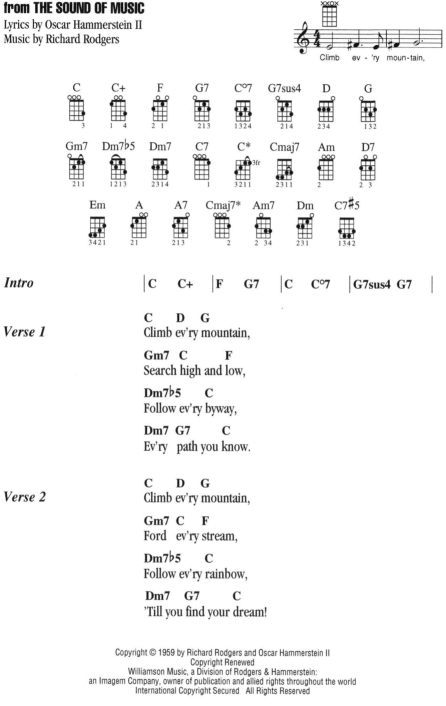

Intro

| C C+ | F G7 | C C°7 | G7sus4 G7 |

Verse 1

C   D   G
Climb ev'ry mountain,

Gm7 C   F
Search high and low,

Dm7♭5   C
Follow ev'ry byway,

Dm7 G7   C
Ev'ry path you know.

Verse 2

C   D   G
Climb ev'ry mountain,

Gm7 C   F
Ford ev'ry stream,

Dm7♭5   C
Follow ev'ry rainbow,

Dm7 G7   C
'Till you find your dream!

Bridge

C7 F
A dream that will need

Dm7   G   C*   Cmaj7 Am
All the love you can give.

D7 G
Ev'ry day of your life

Em   A   D D7
For as long as you live.

Verse 3

G   A7   D
Climb ev'ry mountain,

Dm7 G   Cmaj7*
Ford   ev'ry stream,

Am   Am7 Dm   Dm7
Follow ev'ry rainbow

C   C7♯5 Dm7♭5 G7   C   Dm7 C
'Till you   find   your dream!

Crazy

Words and Music by
Willie Nelson

Melody:

Cra - zy,...

G   E7   Am   D7   D+   G#°7

C   G7   C#°7   A7   Bm

Verse 1

G   E7   Am
Crazy, I'm crazy for feelin' so lonely.

D7   D+   G G#°7 Am D7
I'm crazy, crazy for feelin' so blue.

G   E7   Am
I knew you'd love me as long as you wanted,

D7   G C G G7
And then someday you'd leave me for somebody new.

Bridge

C   C#°7   G
Worry? Why do I let myself worry,

A7   D7 Am D7
Wonderin' what in the world did I do?

Verse 2

G   E7   Am
Oh, crazy for thinkin' that my love could hold you.

C   Bm   Am   G#°7
I'm crazy for tryin' and crazy for cryin'

Am   D7   G
And I'm crazy for lovin' you.

Edelweiss

from THE SOUND OF MUSIC

Lyrics by Oscar Hammerstein II
Music by Richard Rodgers

E - del - weiss,

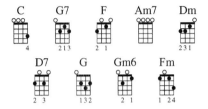

Verse

C   G7   C   F
Edel - weiss, edel - weiss,

C   Am7   Dm G7
Ev'ry morning you greet me.

C   G7   C   F
Small and white, clean and bright.

C   G7   C
You look happy to meet me.

Bridge

G7
Blossom of snow,

        C
May you bloom and grow,

F   D7   G G7
Bloom and grow for - ev - er.

Outro

C   Gm6 F   Fm
Edel - weiss, edel - weiss,

C   G7   C
Bless my homeland for - ever.

Emily

from the MGM Motion Picture
THE AMERICANIZATION OF EMILY
Music by Johnny Mandel
Words by Johnny Mercer

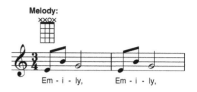

Melody:

Em - i - ly,   Em - i - ly,

Cmaj7 Am7 Dm7 G7 C Gm7 C7♭9 F

Fm6 A F#m7 Bm7 E7♭9 D7 G7#5♭9 D♭7♭5

C7 C7#5 F+ F6 Am D6 B7#5♭9 B7♭9

Em7 A9 C#°7 G7#5 A7#5 D♭ A7#5♭9 C⁶₉

Verse 1

Cmaj7 Am7 Dm7
Emily, Emily, Emily

G7   C   Am7
Has the mur-mur - ing

Gm7 C7♭9 F   Fm6
Sound ___ of May.

A   F#m7
All silver bells, coral shells,

Bm7   E7♭9
Carousels and the

Am7   D7   Dm7 G7#5♭9
Laughter of children at play   say

Verse 2

Cmaj7 Am7 Dm7
Emily,   Emily, Emily,

G7   Cmaj7 D♭7♭5
And we fade to a

C7 C7#5   F F+ F6
Mar - velous view.

Bm7 E7♭9 Am D6
Two _____ lov - ers

Am7 B7#5♭9 B7♭9 Em7   A9
A - lone   and out of sight

C#°7 Dm7
See - ing   images

G7 G7#5 Em7   A9
In the firelight.

A7#5 Am7 G7   Dm7 D♭
As my   eyes vis - ual - ize

Fm6 Em7 A9   A7#5♭9
A family ___ they see

Dm7   G7   G7#5 C C§
Dreamily, Emily _____ too.

Fly Me to the Moon
(In Other Words)

Words and Music by
Bart Howard

Am7   Dm7   G7   Cmaj7   Fmaj7   Bm7♭5   E7   A7   Em7♭5   Dm7♭5

Verse 1

Am7   Dm7   G7   Cmaj7
Fly me to the moon, and let me play among the stars,
Fmaj7   Bm7♭5   E7   Am7
Let me see what spring is like on Jupiter and Mars.
A7 Dm7   G7   Cmaj7 A7
In   other words, ___ hold my hand!
Dm7   G7   Bm7♭5 Dm7 G7
In other words, ___ darling, kiss me.

Verse 2

Am7   Dm7   G7   Cmaj7
Fill my heart with song, and let me sing you forever - more.
Fmaj7   Bm7♭5   E7   Am7
You are all I long for, all I worship and a - dore.
A7 Dm7   G7   Em7♭5 A7
In   other words, ___ please be true.
Dm7   G7   Cmaj7 Dm7♭5 G7
In other words, ___ I love you.

Verse 3   *Repeat Verse 1*

Verse 4

Am7   Dm7   G7   Cmaj7
Fill my heart with song, and let me sing you forever - more.
Fmaj7   Bm7♭5   E7   Am7
You are all I long for, all I worship and a - dore.
A7 Dm7   G7   Em7♭5 A7
In   other words, ___ please be true.
Dm7   G7   Cmaj7
In other words, ___ I love you.

Isn't It Romantic?

from the Paramount Picture
LOVE ME TONIGHT

Words by Lorenz Hart
Music by Richard Rodgers

Melody: I've nev-er met you, yet nev-er

Ab Abm Eb Bb7 Fm7 Gb°7 Bb7#5 Ebmaj7 C7 Eb6

F7 C7#5 Fm G7 Cm G7#5 Eb7 F9 Abm6 E°7

Intro | Ab Abm | Eb | Bb7 |

Prelude
Fm7 Bb7   Ab
      I've never met you,

Abm   Eb
Yet never doubt, dear,

Gb°7   Fm7
I can't forget ___ you,

Bb7#5   Ebmaj7
I've thought you out, dear.

    Ab   Bb7   Eb
I know your profile and I know the way you kiss,

C7   Fm7 Bb7   Eb
Just the thing I miss on a night like this.

    Ab Abm   Eb
If dreams are made of imagi - nation,

Gb°7   Fm7 Bb7#5   Ebmaj7
I'm not a - fraid of my own cre - ation.

    Ab   Bb7   Eb
With all my heart, my heart is here for you to take.

Gb°7   Bb7 Eb6 F7 Bb7
Why should I quake? I'm not a - wake.

$$E\flat$$
Isn't it ro - mantic?

B$\flat$7   E$\flat$ B$\flat$7$\sharp$5 E$\flat$
Music in the night, a dream that can be heard.

B$\flat$7   E$\flat$
Isn't it ro - mantic?

B$\flat$7   E$\flat$ C7$\sharp$5 C7
Moving shadows write the oldest magic word.

Fm B$\flat$7   G7
I   hear the breezes playing

Cm G7$\sharp$5 Cm E$\flat$7
In the trees a - bove

A$\flat$ C7 Fm7   B$\flat$7
While ___ all the world is saying

Cm   F9   G$\flat$°7
You were meant for love.

B$\flat$7   E$\flat$
Isn't it ro - mantic?

B$\flat$7   E$\flat$ B$\flat$7$\sharp$5 E$\flat$
Merely to be young on such a night as this?

B$\flat$7   E$\flat$
Isn't it ro - mantic?

B$\flat$7   E$\flat$ C7$\sharp$5 C7
Ev'ry note that's sung is like a lover's kiss.

Fm B$\flat$7   G7
Sweet symbols in the moonlight,

Cm   E$\flat$6   F9
Do you mean that I

   A$\flat$m6 E$\flat$ E°7   B$\flat$7
Will fall in love perchance?

         E$\flat$ G$\flat$°7
Isn't it ro - mance?

Verse 2

B♭7   E♭
Isn't it ro - mantic?

B♭7   E♭   B♭7#5 E♭
Soon I will have found some girl that I a - dore.

B♭7   E♭
Isn't it ro - mantic?

B♭7   E♭   C7#5 C7
While I sit around, my love can scrub the floor.

Fm B♭7   G7
She'll kiss me ev'ry hour

Cm   G7#5 Cm E♭7
Or she'll get the sack.

A♭ C7 Fm   B♭7
And ___ when I take a shower

Cm   F9   B♭°7
She can scrub my back.

B♭7   E♭
Isn't it ro - mantic?

B♭7   E♭   B♭7#5 E♭
On a moonlight night she'll cook me onion soup.

B♭7   E♭
Kiddies are ro - mantic,

B♭7   E♭   C7#5 C7
And if we don't fight, we soon will have a troupe!

Fm B♭7   G7
We'll help the popu - lation,

Cm E♭6 F9   A♭m6
It's a duty that we owe

  E♭ E°7   B♭7
To dear old France.

        E♭   A♭m6 E♭6
Isn't it ro - mance?

Georgia on My Mind

Words by Stuart Gorrell
Music by Hoagy Carmichael

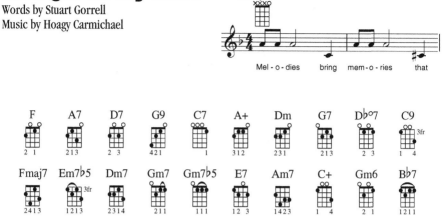

Melody:

Mel - o - dies bring mem - o - ries that

F A7 D7 G9 C7 A+ Dm G7 D♭°7 C9

Fmaj7 Em7♭5 Dm7 Gm7 Gm7♭5 E7 Am7 C+ Gm6 B♭7

Verse 1

     F   A7
Melodies bring memories

     D7   G9 C7
That linger in my heart.

     F   A+ A7/D Dm
Make me think of   Geor - gia,

     G7   D♭°7 C9 F C7
Why did we ev - er part?

     F   A7
Some sweet day when blossoms fall

     D7   G9 C7
And all the world's a song,

     F   A+ A7/D Dm
I'll go back to   Geor - gia

     G7   D♭°7 C7 F
'Cause that's where I   be - long.

UKULELE CHORD SONGBOOK

Chorus

Fmaj7 Em7♭5 A7 Dm7   Gm7
Georgia, Georgia, ___ the whole day through.

Gm7♭5 Fmaj7 E7   Gm7 C7 Am7 D7
Just an old sweet song keeps Georgia on my mind.

Gm7   C+
(Georgia on my mind.)

Fmaj7 Em7♭5 A7 Dm7   Gm7
Georgia, Georgia, ___ a song of you

Gm7♭5 Fmaj7 E7   Gm7   C7   F Gm7♭5 F A7
Comes as sweet and clear as moonlight through the pines.

Bridge

Dm7   Gm6   Dm7 B♭7
Other arms ___ reach out to me,

Dm7   Gm6   Dm7 G7
Other eyes ___ smile tenderly.

Dm7   Gm6 Dm7   E7
Still in peace - ful dreams I see

  Am7   D7   Gm7 C7
The road leads back to you.

Outro

Fmaj7 Em7♭5 A7 Dm7   Gm7
Georgia, Georgia, ___ no peace I find.

Gm7♭5 Fmaj7 E7   Gm7 C7 Fmaj7
Just an old sweet song keeps Georgia on my mind.

The Girl from Ipanema
(Garôta de Ipanema)

Music by Antonio Carlos Jobim
English Words by Norman Gimbel
Original Words by Vinicius de Moraes

Melody:

Tall   and tan and   young _   and love - ly,

Fmaj7   G7   Gm7   Gb7b5   F#maj7   B7

F#m7   D7   Eb7   Am7   D7b9   C7b9

Verse 1

Fmaj7
Tall and tan and young and lovely,

G7
The girl ___ from Ipanema goes walking,

Gm7
And when ___ she passes,

Gb7b5   **Fmaj7 Gb7b5**
Each one ___ she passes goes   "Ah!"

Verse 2

Fmaj7
When she walks she's like a samba

G7
That swings ___ so cool and sways so gentle,

Gm7
That when ___ she passes,

Gb7b5   **Fmaj7**
Each one ___ she passes goes   "Ah!"

Bridge

F#maj7   B7
Oh, but I watch her so sadly.

F#m7   D7
How ___ can I tell her I love her?

Gm7   Eb7
Yes, ___ I would give my heart gladly,

Am7   D7b9
But each day when she walks to the sea

Gm7   C7b9
She looks straight ahead not at me.

Verse 3

Fmaj7
Tall and tan and young and lovely,

G7
The girl ___ from Ipanema goes walking,

Gm7
And when ___ she passes,

Gb7b5   Fmaj7
I smile, ___ but she doesn't see.

Gb7b5   Fmaj7
She just doesn't see.

Gb7b5   Fmaj7
No, she doesn't see.

Here's That Rainy Day

from CARNIVAL IN FLANDERS

Words by Johnny Burke
Music by Jimmy Van Heusen

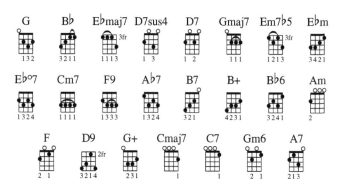

Melody:

May - be I should have saved those

Intro

| G | B♭ | E♭maj7 | D7sus4 D7 |

Verse 1

Gmaj7 B♭   Em7♭5
Maybe I should have saved

E♭maj7 E♭m E♭°7
Those left over dreams.

D7sus4   D7   E♭°7 G
Funny, but here's that rainy day.

Chorus

Cm7 F9 A♭7
Here's that rainy day

B7 B♭ B+ B♭6
They told me a - bout,

 Am   F
And I laughed at the thought

  D9   G
That it might turn out this way.

Verse 2

Gmaj7 B♭ Em7♭5
Where is that worn out wish

 E♭maj7 E♭m E♭°7
That I threw a - side

D7sus4 D7   E♭°7 G G+
After it brought my lover near?

Cmaj7 C7   D7
Funny, ____ how love becomes

 G Gm6 A7
A cold rainy day.

D7sus4 D7   G B♭ E♭maj7 D7sus4 G
Funny, that rainy day is here.

How Deep Is the Ocean
(How High Is the Sky)

Words and Music by
Irving Berlin

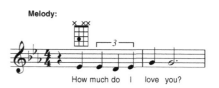

Melody:

How much do I love you?

Eb	F9	Bb7	G7#5	G7	Cm	G+	Am7b5	Gm	D7
2341	1333	1324 (3fr)	312	213	3111	231	1312	231 (5fr)	1112

Bb9	Eb7	Ab9	F7b9	F7	Bb7#5	C7	Fm	Fm7b5	Eb6
2143	1112	1 32	1324	2314	1342	1	1 24	1312	1111

Intro |Eb |F9 |Bb7 |Eb G7#5 G7 |

Verse 1

    Cm   G+
How much do I love you?

Cm   Am7b5
I'll tell you no lie,

Gm   D7
How deep is the ocean,

Gm   Bb9
How high is the sky?

Eb   Eb7   Ab9
How many times a day do I think of you?

F7b9 F7   Bb7#5 Bb7   G7
How many roses are sprin - kled with dew?

Verse 2

Cm   **G+**
How far would I travel

Cm   **Am7♭5**
To be where you are?

Gm   **D7**
How far is the journey

Gm   **B♭9**
From here to a star?

E♭ **C7**
And if I ever lost you,

Fm   **Fm7♭5**
How much would I cry?

E♭   **F9**
How deep is the ocean,

B♭7   **E♭ E♭6**
How high is the sky?

I Dreamed a Dream
from LES MISÉRABLES

Music by Claude-Michel Schönberg
Lyrics by Alain Boublil, Jean-Marc Natel
and Herbert Kretzmer

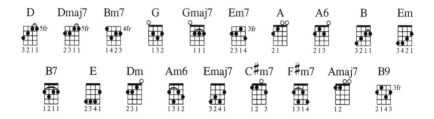

Melody:

I dreamed a dream in time gone by

D   Dmaj7   Bm7   G   Gmaj7   Em7   A   A6   B   Em

B7   E   Dm   Am6   Emaj7   C#m7   F#m7   Amaj7   B9

Verse 1

> **D   Dmaj7   Bm7 D**
> I dreamed a dream in time gone by
>
> **G   Gmaj7   Em7 A**
> When hope was high and life worth living.
>
> **D   Dmaj7   Bm7 D**
> I dreamed that love would never die.
>
> **G   Gmaj7   Em7 A**
> I dreamed that God would be for - giving.

Verse 2

> **D   Dmaj7   Bm7 D**
> Then I was young and unafraid
>
> **G   Gmaj7   Em7 A6**
> And dreams were made and used and wasted.
>
> **D   Dmaj7   Bm7 D**
> There was no ransom to be paid,
>
> **G   Gmaj7   Em7 A**
> No song un - sung, no wine un - tasted.

Bridge

```
B                 Em
But the tigers come at night

B      B7         E
With their voices soft as thunder.

A                      Dm
As they tear your hope a - part,

A                         D Em7 D G A
As they turn your dream to shame.
```

Verse 3

```
D         Dmaj7      Bm7 D
He slept a summer by my side.

G          Gmaj7         Em7   A6
He filled my days with endless wonder.

D         Dmaj7      Bm7 D
He took my childhood in his stride.

G          A6              D     A Am6 B
But he was gone when autumn came.
```

Verse 4

```
E         Emaj7          C♯m7 E
And still I dreamed he'd come to me,

A           Amaj7       F♯m7 B
That we would live the years to - gether.

E         Emaj7          C♯m7 E
But there are dreams that cannot be,

A           Amaj7       F♯m7 B E
And there are storms we cannot weather.

C♯m7   E              A Amaj7
I had a dream my life would be

F♯m7      A     B    E
So diff'rent from this hell I'm living,

          Emaj7     C♯m7 E
So diff'rent now from what it seemed.

A         B
Now life has killed the dream I dreamed.
```

Outro

```
|E  Emaj7  |C♯m7 E   |A  B9  |E      |
```

I Left My Heart in San Francisco

Words by Douglass Cross
Music by George Cory

Melody:

The love - li - ness of

Cm7 F7 B♭maj7 B♭§ F9 D7♭9 Gm Gm(maj7) C9sus4

C9 F9sus4 Cm7♭5 Gm7♭5 G♭9 F D7 C#°7 B♭m6 C6

Am7 Gm7 C7♭9 B°7 E♭6 D D7* G7#5 G7 B9

Intro | Cm7 | F7 | B♭maj7 | B♭§ |

| | Cm7 F7   B♭maj7 |
Prelude | The loveli - ness of Paris |

B♭§   Cm7   F7 B♭maj7
Seems somehow sadly gay.

B♭§   F9   D7♭9   Gm Gm(maj7)
The glory that was Rome

C9sus4 C9   F9sus4
Is of an - other day.

F9   Cm7♭5
I've been terribly alone

Gm7♭5   G♭9
And for - gotten in Man - hattan.

F   D7   C9sus4 C9   F9sus4 F9
I'm going home to my city   by the bay.

Verse 1

Cm7 C#°7 B♭maj7
I left   my   heart

C#°7   Cm7
In San Fran - cisco.

F9sus4 F9   B♭maj7 Cm7
High on a hill, it   calls to me.

B♭maj7 Cm7 C#°7 B♭maj7
To   be   where little cable cars

B♭m6   C6   Am7
Climb halfway to the stars.

D7♭9 Gm7 C9   C7♭9 F9sus4 F9
The morning fog ____ may chill the air,

B°7   Cm7
I don't care.

Verse 2

F7 C#°7 B♭maj7
My love waits there

C#°7   Cm7
In San Fran - cisco,

F7   E♭6   D
Above the blue and windy sea.

D7*   G7#5 G7   C9
When I come home to you, San Fran - cisco,

B9   C9 F9sus4
Your gold - en   sun

Cm7 B9 B♭§
Will shine for me.

I'll Be Seeing You

Written by Irving Kahal
and Sammy Fain

Melody:
I'll be see-ing you _ in all _ the old _

Gmaj7 B7 Am7 Am(maj7) D7 Em7 D9 Dm7♯5 D7♯5 E7♭9

C♯m7♭5 F♯m7♭5 Dm6 E7 Em Em(maj7) Am7♭5 Dm7 G7♯5 G

Verse 1

Gmaj7 B7　　Am7　　　Am(maj7) Am7　　Am(maj7)
I'll be seeing you　in all the old　　　familiar places

Am7　Am(maj7) D7　　　Gmaj7
That this heart of　mine embraces all day through.

Em7　　　　Am7
In that small café,　the park across the way,

D9　　　　Dm7♯5　　D7♯5
The children's ___ carousel,

　Gmaj7　　E7♭9　C♯m7♭5 F♯m7♭5
The chestnut trees, ___ the wishing　well.

Verse 2

      Gmaj7 B7   **Am7 Am(maj7) Am7**   **Am(maj7)**
      I'll be   seeing you   in ev'ry lovely summer's day,

      Am7   **D9**   **D7**
      In ev'rything that's light and gay.

      Dm6   **E7**
      I'll always think of you that way,

      Am7   **B7**
      I'll find you in the morning sun.

      Em   **Em(maj7) C♯m7♭5**
      And when the night is   new,

      Am7   **Am7♭5 D7**
      I'll be looking at the moon,   but I'll be seeing you.

Interlude

      | **Gmaj7** | **B7** | **Am7 Am(maj7)** | **Am7 Am(maj7)** |
      | **Am7** | **D9** | **Dm7** | **G7♯5** |

Outro

      Am7   **Am(maj7) F♯m7♭5 B7**
      I'll ____ find you in the morning sun.

      Em   **Em7 C♯m7♭5 Am7**
      When the night is new, I'll be looking at the moon,

      Am7♭5   **G**
      But, I'll be seeing you.

Imagine

Written by
John Lennon

Melody:

Im - ag - ine there's   no   heav - en.

C   Cmaj7   F   Dm   G   G6sus4   G7   E   E7

Intro

‖: C   Cmaj7 | F   :‖

Verse 1

C   Cmaj7   F
Imagine there's no heaven.

C   Cmaj7   F
It's easy if you __ try.

C   Cmaj7   F
No hell below us,

C   Cmaj7   F
Above us only sky.

Pre-Chorus 1

F   C   Dm
Imagine all __ the peo - ple

G   G6sus4   G7
Living for today.

Verse 2

C   Cmaj7   F
Imagine there's no countries.

C   Cmaj7   F
It isn't hard to do.

C   Cmaj7   F
Nothing to kill or die __ for

C   Cmaj7   F
And no religion, __ too.

Pre-Chorus 2

```
F              C          Dm
Imagine all __ the peo - ple

G        G6sus4   G7
Living life in peace.
```

Chorus 1

```
F        G        C       Cmaj7  E  E7
You, __ you may say I'm a dreamer.

F        G              C Cmaj7  E  E7
But I'm not the only one.

F            G        C       Cmaj7  E  E7
I hope some day you'll join us

F        G        C
And the world will be as one.
```

Verse 3

```
C           Cmaj7       F
Imagine no possessions.

C            Cmaj7    F
I wonder if you __ can.

C                   Cmaj7  F
No need for greed or hunger,

C             Cmaj7    F
A brotherhood of __ man.
```

Pre-Chorus 3

```
F            C          Dm
Imagine all __ the peo - ple

G        G6sus4    G7
Sharing all the world.
```

Chorus 2

```
F        G        C       Cmaj7  E  E7
You, __ you may say I'm a dreamer.

F        G              C Cmaj7  E  E7
But I'm not the only one.

F            G        C       Cmaj7  E  E7
I hope some day you'll join us

F        G        C
And the world will live as one.
```

In the Wee Small Hours of the Morning

Words by Bob Hilliard
Music by David Mann

Melody:

When the sun is high in the

Cmaj7 G7 Em7 B7♭9 A7♭9 D7 C7 C6

C+ Dm7 Em7♭5 A7 F♯m7♭5 B7 D♯°7 A♭7♭5

Verse

     Cmaj7 G7 **Cmaj7 G7**
When the sun is high in the afternoon sky,

     Cmaj7 **G7** **Cmaj7**
You can always find something to do.

     Em7 **B7♭9** **Em7** **B7♭9**
But from dusk till dawn as the clock ticks on,

Em7   **A7♭9** **D7 G7**
Something hap - pens to you.

Chorus 1

```
        Cmaj7    C7          C6
In the wee small hours of the morning,

C+         Cmaj7 C+           Dm7 G7
While the whole  world is fast a - sleep,

Dm7 G7        Em7♭5        A7
You lie a - wake and think about the girl,

F♯m7♭5  B7            Em7
And never ever think of counting sheep.

G7          Cmaj7  C7              C6
When your lonely   heart has learned its lesson,

C+         Cmaj7 Em7♭5       A7
You'd be hers if   only she would call.

    Dm7       D♯°7      Em7
In the wee small hours of the morning,

A7        Dm7             G7    C6
That's the time you miss her most of all.
```

Chorus 2

```
        Cmaj7    C7          C6
In the wee small hours of the morning,

C+         Cmaj7 C+           Dm7 G7
While the whole   world is fast a - sleep,

Dm7 G7        Em7♭5        A7
You lie a  - wake and think about the girl,

F♯m7♭5  B7            Em7
And never ever think of counting sheep.

G7          Cmaj7  C7              C6
When your lonely   heart has learned its lesson,

C+         Cmaj7 Em7♭5       A7
You'd be hers if   only she would call.

    Dm7       D♯°7      Em7
In the wee small hours of the morning,

A7        Dm7             A♭7♭5  G7  C6
That's the time you miss her most   of   all.
```

It Might as Well Be Spring

from STATE FAIR

Lyrics by Oscar Hammerstein II
Music by Richard Rodgers

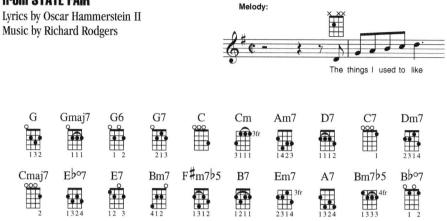

G	Gmaj7	G6	G7	C	Cm	Am7	D7	C7	Dm7
132	111	1 2	213	3111	1423 3fr	1112		1	2314

Cmaj7	E♭°7	E7	Bm7	F♯m7♭5	B7	Em7	A7	Bm7♭5	B♭°7
2	1324	12 3	412	1312	1211	2314 3fr	1324	1333 4fr	1 2

Intro

        G   Gmaj7 G6   G
The things I used to like I   don't like any - more.

        Gmaj7   G6   G7
I want a lot of other things I've never had be - fore.

        C   Cm   G   Am7 D7   G
It's just like Mother says, I "sit a - round and mope"

        C   Cm G   Am7   D7   G
Pre - tending I am wonderful and knowing I'm a dope.

Verse 1

        Gmaj7   C7   Gmaj7
I'm as restless as a willow in a windstorm,

C7   Gmaj7   Dm7
I'm as jumpy as a puppet on a string.

G7 Cmaj7 E♭°7   Gmaj7
I'd say that I had spring fever,

E7   Am7   D7 Bm7 E7 Am7
But I know it isn't spring.

Verse 2

D7 Gmaj7　　　C7　　　　　　Gmaj7
I am starry eyed and vaguely discon - tented,

C7　　Gmaj7　　　　　　　　Dm7
Like a nightingale without a song to sing.

G7　Cmaj7　　　Eb°7　　　Gmaj7
Oh, why should I have spring - fever,

E7　　　　Am7 D7　Gmaj7 Dm7 G7
When it isn't　even spring?

Bridge

Cmaj7 Am7　　　　Dm7　　　G7
I keep　wishing I were somewhere else

Dm7　　　　　G7　　　Cmaj7
Walking down a strange new street.

Am7　Am7　　　　　　F#m7b5 B7
Hearing words that I have never　　heard

　　　Em7　　A7　Am7
From a man I've yet to meet.

Verse 3

D7　　Gmaj7 C7　　　　Gmaj7
I'm as busy as a spider spinning daydreams,

C7　　Gmaj7　　　　　　Dm7
I'm as giddy as a baby on a swing.

G7 Cmaj7　　　Eb°7　　Gmaj7
I haven't seen a crocus or a rosebud,

E7　　Am7 D7　Bm7b5
Or a robin on the wing.

E7　　A7　　　　Am7　　　D7
But I feel so gay in a melancholy way

　　Bm7　Em7　A7
That it might as well be spring.

Bb°7 Bm7 Em7 Am7　D7 Gmaj7
It might as　well　be　spring!

Just the Way You Are

Words and Music
by Billy Joel

Melody:

Don't go ___ chang-ing ___

D   Gm6   G5   Bm6   Gmaj7   Bm7   D7   Gm7   Am7   Em7

E7   Gadd2   E9   A   F#m7   B7   Dmaj7   C   Bb

Intro

‖: D   Gm6   D   G5 | D   Gm6   D   G5   :‖

Verse 1

D   Bm6   Gmaj7   Bm7   D7
Don't go changing   to try and please ___ me.

Gmaj7   Gm7   D Am7   D7
You never let me down before.   Mm.

Gmaj7   Gm7   D   Bm7
I don't imag - ine   you're too famil - iar

Em7   E7   Gadd2
And I don't see you anymore.

Verse 2

D   Bm6   Gmaj7   Bm7 D7
I ___ would not leave you   in times of trouble.

Gmaj7   Gm7   D Am7 D7
We never could have come this far.   Mm.

Gmaj7   Gm7   D   Bm7
I took the good times;   I'll take the bad times.

Em7   Gadd2
I'll take you just the way you are.

| D   Gm6   D   G5 | D   Gm6   D   G5 |

Verse 3

D   Bm6 Gmaj7   Bm7   D7
Don't go trying   some new fash - ion,

Gmaj7   Gm7   D Am7   D7
Don't change the color of your hair.   Mm.

Gmaj7   Gm7   D   Bm7
You always have my   unspoken pas - sion,

                    E9   Gadd2
Although I might ___ not seem to care.

     D   Bm6 Gmaj7   Bm7   D7
I ___ don't want clever   conversa - tion;

Gmaj7 Gm7   D Am7   D7
I never want to work that hard.   Mm.

Gmaj7   Gm7   D   Bm7
I just want someone   that I can talk to.

Em7   Gadd2
I want you just ___ the way you are.

|D Gm6 D G5 |D Gm6 D D7 |

Bridge

Gmaj7   A   F#m7   B7
I need to know ___ that you will al - ways be

Em7   Gadd2   Dmaj7
The same old someone that I ___ knew.

    C B♭   C   Am7   D7
Oh, _____ what will it take till you believe ___ in me

Gm7   Gadd2
The way that I believe in you?

Verse 4

```
          D       Bm6    Gmaj7           Bm7   D7
          I __ said I love you    and that's for - ever,
```

```
          Gmaj7    Gm7                  D  Am7   D7
          And this I promise from the heart.    Mm.
```

```
          Gmaj7      Gm7    D      Bm7
          I couldn't love you    any bet - ter.
```

```
          Em7              Gadd2
          I love you just ___ the way you are.
```

```
          |D    Gm6   D    G5  |D   Gm6   D   G5    |
```

Sax Solo

```
          |D       Bm6  |Gmaj7 Bm7  D7 |Gmaj7 Gm7  |D        Am7 D7 |
          |Gmaj7 Gm7  |D       Bm7        |      E9  |Gadd2          |
```

Verse 5

```
          D           Bm6 Gmaj7      Bm7    D7
          I ___ don't want clever    conver - sation;
```

```
          Gmaj7   Gm7                  D  Am7   D7
          I never want to work that hard.    Mm.
```

```
          Gmaj7     Gm7    D              Bm7
          I just want someone    that I can talk ___ to;
```

```
          Em7              Gadd2
          I want you just ___ the way you are.
```

```
          |B♭   C   |Am7   D7   |Gm7  Gadd2   |
```

Outro

```
          ||:D    Bm6    |Gmaj7  Bm7  D7 |Gmaj7  Gm7      |
          |D    Am7 D7 |Gmaj7  Gm7      |D        Bm7    |
          |      E7    |Gadd2            :||  Repeat and fade
```

Let It Be

Words and Music by
John Lennon and Paul McCartney

Melody:

When I   find __ my - self __ in   times of   trou - ble...

C   G   Am   F   G6   Fmaj7

Verse 1

    C   G
When I find myself in times of trouble

Am F
Mother Mary comes to me

C   G
Speaking words of wis - dom,

  F C
Let it be.

       G
And in my hour of dark - ness

   Am   F
She is standing right in front of me

C   G
Speaking words of wisdom,

  F C
Let it be.

Chorus 1

     Am G6
Let it be, __ let it be,

     Fmaj7 C
Ah, let it be, __ let it be.

       G
Whisper words of wisdom,

  F C
Let it be.

Verse 2

       C   **G**
And when the broken heart - ed people

Am   **F**
Living in the world __ agree,

C   **G**
There will be an an - swer,

  F **C**
Let it be.

           G
For though they may be part - ed there is

Am   **F**
Still a chance that they __ will see

C   **G**
There will be an an-swer,

  F **C**
Let it be.

Chorus 2

     Am   **G6**
Let it be, __ let it be,

      Fmaj7 **C**
Ah, let it be, __ let it be.

         G
Yeah, there will be an an - swer,

  F **C**
Let it be.

Verse 3

        C   G
And when the night is cloud - y

         Am   F
There is still a light that shines on me;

        C   G
Shine until tomor - row,

         F   C
Let it be.

                       G
I wake up to the sound __ of music;

Am   F
Mother Mary comes __ to me,

C   G
Speaking words of wisdom,

     F   C
Let it be.

Chorus 3

            Am   G6
Let it be, __ let it be,

              Fmaj7   C
Ah, let it be, __ let it be.

                     G
Yeah, there will be an - swer,

     F   C
Let it be.

         Am   G6
Let it be, __ let it be,

          Fmaj7   C
Ah, let it be, __ let it be.

                  G
Whisper words of wisdom,

     F   C   F   C   G   F   C
Let it be.

The Lady Is a Tramp

from BABES IN ARMS
from WORDS AND MUSIC

Words by Lorenz Hart
Music by Richard Rodgers

Melody:

I get too hun-gry

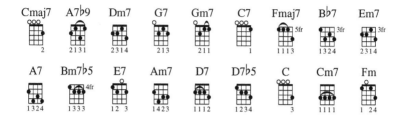

Cmaj7 A7♭9 Dm7 G7 Gm7 C7 Fmaj7 B♭7 Em7

A7 Bm7♭5 E7 Am7 D7 D7♭5 C Cm7 Fm

Verse 1

Cmaj7   A7♭9   Dm7   G7
I get too hungry for dinner at eight,

Cmaj7   A7♭9   Dm7   G7
I like the theater but never come late.

Cmaj7 Gm7 C7   Fmaj7   B♭7
I never bother ___ with people I hate,

Em7   A7   Dm7 G7 Cmaj7 Dm7 G7
That's why the lady   is a tramp.

Verse 2

Cmaj7 A7♭9   Dm7   G7
I don't like crap-games with barons and earls,

Cmaj7 A7♭9 Em7   G7
Won't go to Harlem in ermine and pearls.

Cmaj7   Gm7 C7   Fmaj7 B♭7
Won't dish the dirt _____ with the rest of the girls,

Em7 A7 Dm7 G7 Cmaj7
That's why the lady is a tramp.

Bridge

      Dm7 G7 Em7   A7
I like the free fresh wind in my hair,

Dm7   G7
Life without care.

Em7   A7 Dm7 G7
I'm broke, ____ it's oke.

Outro

Cmaj7 A7♭9 Dm7   Bm7♭5 E7
Hate Cali - fornia, it's cold and it's damp.

Am7   D7 D7♭5 G7 C Cm7 Dm7 Fm G7 C
That's why the lady is a tramp.

Long Ago (And Far Away)

from COVER GIRL
Words by Ira Gershwin
Music by Jerome Kern

Melody:

Long a - go and far

G6 Em7 Am7 D7 Gmaj7 Bm7 E7 B♭6 Gm7 Cm7

F7 B♭maj7 A7 Dmaj7 Dm7 G7 Cmaj7 F9 B♭°7

Verse 1

G6 Em7 Am7 D7 Gmaj7
Long ___ a - go and far a - way,

Am7 D7 G6
I dreamed a dream one day.

Am7 D7 Bm7 E7 Am7 D7
And now ___ that dream is here be - side me.

Bridge

B♭6 Gm7 Cm7 F7 B♭maj7
Long ___ the skies were over - cast,

A7 Dmaj7
But now the clouds have passed.

Bm7 E7 Am7 D7
You're here at last!

Verse 2

G6 Em7 Am7 D7 Gmaj7
Chills ___ run up and down my spine,

Am7 D7 G6
A - laddin's lamp is mine,

Am7 D7 Bm7 E7 Am7 D7
The dream ___ I dreamed was not de - nied me.

Outro

Dm7 G7 Cmaj7
Just one look and then I knew,

F9 G6 B♭°7 Am7 D7 G6
That all I longed ___ for, long a - go, was you.

Moon River

from the Paramount Picture
BREAKFAST AT TIFFANY'S

Words by Johnny Mercer
Music by Henry Mancini

Melody:

Moon   Riv - er,   wid - er than a

C   Am   F   Bm7♭5   E7   C7   B♭9   F♯m7♭5   B7

Em7   A7   Dm7   G9   F9   A♭maj7   D♭maj7   C6/9

Intro | C | |

Verse 1
C   Am   F   C
Moon River, wider than a mile;

F   C   Bm7♭5 E7
I'm crossin' you in style some - day.

Am   C7   F   B♭9
Old dream maker, you heart breaker,

Am   F♯m7♭5 B7
Wher - ever you're goin',

Em7 A7   Dm7 G9
I'm goin' ____ your way.

Verse 2
C   Am   F   C
Two drifters, off to see the world.

F   C   Bm7♭5 E7
There's such a lot of world to see.

Am   F♯m7♭5 F9   C
We're after the same   rainbows end.

F   C   F   C
Waitin' 'round the bend,   my Huckleberry friend,

Am   Dm7   A♭maj7 D♭maj7 C6/8
Moon River and me.

Love Me Tender

Words and Music by Elvis Presley
and Vera Matson

Melody:

Love me _____ ten-der,

D E7 A7 F# Bm D7 G Gm F#°7 B7

Intro
| D |

Verse 1

D   E7
Love me tender,   love me sweet.

A7   D
   Never let me go.

                        E7
You have made my life __ complete,

A7   D
And I love you so.

Chorus 1

D   F#
Love me tender,

Bm   D7
   Love me true.

G   Gm   D
All my dreams ful - fill.

  F#°7 B7   E7
For, my   darlin',   I love you,

A7   D
And I always will.

Verse 2

```
          D              E7
Love me tender, love me long.

A7                   D
Take me to your heart.

                   E7
For it's there that I __ belong,

A7              D
And we'll never part.
```

Chorus 2   *Repeat Chorus 1*

Verse 3

```
          D              E7
Love me tender,    love me, dear.

A7              D
Tell me you are mine.

                        E7
I'll be yours through all __ the years,

A7              D
Till the end of time.
```

Chorus 3

```
          D      F♯
Love me tender,

Bm              D7
    Love me true.

      G    Gm        D
All __ my dreams ful - fill.

      F♯°7 B7      E7
For, my      darling, I love you,

A7              D
And I always will.
```

Love Walked In

Music and Lyrics by
George Gershwin and
Ira Gershwin

Melody:

Noth - ing seemed to   mat - ter   an - y -   more, _____

F9   C9   Bbm7b5   Bb7   Eb   Ebmaj7   E°7   Fm7   G7   Dbm6

F7sus4   F7   Cm   Fm6   G7b5   C7#5   F7b5   Bbm7   Eb7   Abmaj7

Am7   D7   Gmaj7   Bb9   Bb7sus4   Eb+   Ab   C7   Abm6

Intro | F9 | C9 | Bbm7b5 | Bb7 |

Prelude

Eb   Ebmaj7 E°7 Fm7
Nothing seemed to   matter

G7 Dbm6 F7sus4 F7 Cm F7
An - y - more,

Fm7   Fm6
Didn't care what

G7b5 C7#5 F7b5 Bb7 Eb
I   was   head - ed   for.

Bbm7   Eb7 Abmaj7
Time was stand - ing   still.

Am7   D7 Gmaj7 Bb9   Eb
No one count - ed   till _____ there came

Ebmaj7 E°7   Fm7   G7b5
A knock,   knock, knock - ing

F7 Bb7 Eb Fm7 Bb9
At   the   door.

Verse 1

E♭   F7   B♭7sus4   B♭7
Love walked right in and drove the shadows away.

E♭   F7   B♭7
Love walked right in and brought my sunniest day.

E♭   E♭+   A♭   C7♯5
One magic mo - ment and my heart seemed to know

Fm7   C7   Fm7
    That love said, "Hel - lo,"

E♭   A♭   B♭7   F9   B♭7
    Though not a   word was spoken.

Verse 2

E♭   F7   B♭7sus4   B♭7
One look and I for - got the gloom of the past.

E♭   F7   B♭7
One look and I had found my future at last.

E♭   E♭+   A♭   Fm7   A♭m6   E♭
One look and I had   found a world com - pletely   new

     Fm7   B♭7   E♭
When love walked in with you.

Memory

from Cats

Music by Andrew Lloyd Webber
Text by Trevor Nunn after T.S. Eliot

Mid - night, __ not a sound from the pave - ment. __

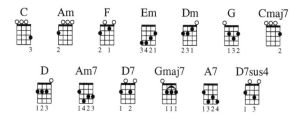

Verse 1

   C   Am
Midnight, not a sound from the pavement.

            F
Has the moon lost her memory?

          Em
She is smiling a - lone.

   Dm   Am
In the lamplight the withered leaves col - lect at my feet

   G   F   C
And the wind be - gins to moan.

Verse 2

   C   Am
Memory, all alone in the moonlight

          F   Em
I can smile at the old days, I was beautiful then.

   Dm   Am
I re - member the time I knew what happiness was,

       G   F   C
Let the memory live a - gain.

UKULELE CHORD SONGBOOK

Bridge 1

Em   Dm
Ev'ry street lamp

Em   Dm
Seems to beat

 Em Cmaj7 D G
A fatal - is - tic warning.

Em   Am7   D7   Gmaj7
Someone mutters and a street lamp gutters

   Em   A7 D
And soon it will be morning.

Verse 3

C   Am
Daylight, I must wait for the sunrise,

               F   Em
I must think of a new life and I mustn't give in.

         Dm   Am
When the dawn comes tonight will be a memory too

   G   F   C
And a new day will be - gin.

Bridge 2

Em   Dm/F
Burned out ends of

Em   Dm
Smoky days,

  Em   C   D7 G
The stale cold smell of morning.

  Em   Am7   D7   Gmaj7
The street lamp dies, another night is over,

  Em A7   D   D7
An - other day is dawning.

Verse 4

C   Am
Touch me, it's so easy to leave me

             F   Em
All alone with the memory of my days in the sun.

   D7sus4   Dm   Am
If you touch me you'll understand what happiness is.

     G   F   C
Look, a new day has be - gun.

Mood Indigo

Words and Music by Duke Ellington,
Irving Mills and Albany Bigard

Melody:

You   ain't been   blue, __

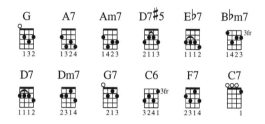

Chorus

     G   **A7**
You ain't been blue,

Am7 D7#5 G
No,   no,   no,

                A7
You ain't been blue,

E♭7   **B♭m7 E♭7 D7**
Till you've had ____ that   mood indigo.

G   **Dm7**   **G7**
  That feelin',   goes ___ stealin',

C6   **F7**   **G**   **A7**
Down to my shoes, while I sit and sigh,

Am7 D7#5 G Am7 D7
"Go   'long blues."

Verse

```
       G              A7
       Always get that mood indigo,

       Am7        D7         G  Am7 D7
       Since my baby said good - bye.

       G              A7
       In the evenin', when lights are low,

       E♭7                    D7
       I'm so lonesome I could cry.

       Dm7                    G7
       'Cause there's nobody who cares about me.

       C7                E♭7            D7
       I'm just a soul who's bluer than blue can ___ be,

       G         A7        Am7        D7        G
       When I get that mood indigo, I could lay me down and die.
```

Moonlight in Vermont

Words by John Blackburn
Music by Karl Suessdorf

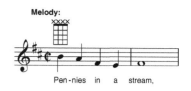

Melody:

Pen‑nies   in   a   stream,

Dmaj7 Bm7 Em7 A7 C7 A♭m7 D♭7 G♭maj7

E♭m7 Am7 D7 Gmaj7 A7♭9 E7 E♭7

Verse 1

Dmaj7 Bm7 Em7 A7
Pennies in a   stream,

Dmaj7 Bm7   C7
Falling   leaves, a sycamore,

Em7   A7   Dmaj7 Em7 A7
Moonlight in Ver - mont.

Verse 2

Dmaj7 Bm7   Em7 A7
Icy   finger - waves,

Dmaj7 Bm7 C7
Ski trails on a   mountainside,

Em7   A7   Dmaj7
Snowlight in Ver - mont.

Bridge

A♭m7   D♭7   G♭maj7   E♭m7
Telegraph ca - bles, they sing down the highway

A♭m7   D♭7   G♭maj7
And travel each bend ____ in the road.

Am7   D7   Gmaj7 Em7
People who meet ____ in this romantic setting

Am7   D7   Gmaj7 A7♭9
Are so hypnotized ____ by the love - ly

Outro

Dmaj7 Bm7   Em7 A7
Evening summer breeze,

Dmaj7 Bm7 C7
Warbling of a   meadowlark,

Em7   A7   Dmaj7 Em7 A7
Moonlight in Ver - mont.

E7   Em7   E♭7   Dmaj7
You and I and moonlight in Ver - mont.

My Favorite Things

from THE SOUND OF MUSIC

Lyrics by Oscar Hammerstein II
Music by Richard Rodgers

Melody:

Rain - drops on ros - es and...

Am   F   Dm   G   C   E7   D7

Verse 1

Am
Raindrops on roses and whiskers on kittens,

F
Bright copper kettles and warm woolen mittens,

Dm   **G**   **C**   **F**
Brown paper packages tied up with strings,

C   **F**   **Dm**   **E7**
These are a few of my favorite things.

Verse 2

Am
Cream-colored ponies and crisp apple strudels,

F
Doorbells and sleigh bells and schnitzel with noodles,

Dm   **G**   **C**   **F**
Wild geese that fly with the moon on their wings,

C   **F**   **Dm**   **E7**
These are a few of my favorite things.

Outro

Am   **E7**
When the dog bites,   when the bee stings,

Am   **F**
When I'm feeling sad,

                D7
I simply remember my favorite things

          C   **F G C   F   C**
And then I don't feel so bad.

My Funny Valentine

from BABES IN ARMS

Words by Lorenz Hart
Music by Richard Rodgers

Melody:

My fun - ny val - en - tine,

Am   Am(maj7)   Am7   Am6   Fmaj7   Dm7   Bm7♭5   E7♭9   Dm7♭5

G7♭9   Cmaj7   Em7   E7   Gm7   F♯7   F♯7♭5   C6

Verse 1

Am   Am(maj7) Am7   Am6
My funny valentine,   sweet comic valentine,
Fmaj7   Dm7   Bm7♭5 E7♭9
You make me smile with my heart.

Am   Am(maj7) Am7   Am6
Your looks are laughable, unphoto - graphable,
Fmaj7   Dm7   Dm7♭5
Yet, you're my fav'rite work of art.

Bridge

G7♭9   Cmaj7 Dm7   Em7
Is your figure   less than Greek?

Dm7 Cmaj7 Dm7 Em7
Is your mouth a little   weak

Dm7   Cmaj7 E7   Am
When you open   it to speak?

Gm7 F♯7 Fmaj7 Bm7♭5
Are   you   smart?

Verse 2

E7♭9   Am   Am(maj7)
But   don't change a hair for me,

Am7   Am6
Not if you care for me.

Fmaj7   Bm7♭5 E7♭9 Am Gm7 F♯7♭5
Stay, little valen - tine,   stay!

Fmaj7   Dm7   G7♭9   C6
Each day is Valen - tine's   Day.

My Way

Melody:

English Words by Paul Anka
Original French Words by Gilles Thibault
Music by Jacques Revaux and
Claude Francois

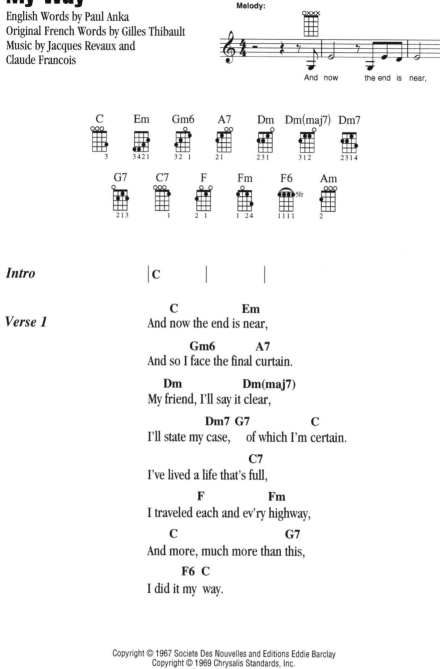

And now   the end is near,

C   Em   Gm6   A7   Dm   Dm(maj7)   Dm7

G7   C7   F   Fm   F6   Am

Intro | C | |

Verse 1
                    C   Em
          And now the end is near,

                    Gm6   A7
          And so I face the final curtain.

                    Dm   Dm(maj7)
          My friend, I'll say it clear,

                    Dm7 G7   C
          I'll state my case,   of which I'm certain.

                              C7
          I've lived a life that's full,

                    F   Fm
          I traveled each and ev'ry highway,

                    C   G7
          And more, much more than this,

                    F6   C
          I did it my way.

Verse 2

         C   **Em**
Re - grets, I've had a few,

        Gm6   **A7**
But then a - gain, too few to mention.

Dm   **Dm(maj7)**
I did what I had to do,

        Dm7 **G7**   **C**
And saw it through   without ex - emption.

                C7
I planned each charted course,

            F   **Fm**
Each careful step along the byway,

      C   **G7**
And more, much more than this,

      F6 **C**
I did it my way.

Bridge

            C   **C7**
Yes, there were times, I'm sure you knew,

       F
When I bit off more than I could chew,

      Dm7   **G7**
But through it all, when there was doubt,

    Em   **Am**
I ate it up and spit it out.

      Dm7   **G7**
I faced it all and I stood tall,

      F6 **C**
And did it my way.

Verse 3

       C   **Em**
I've loved, I've laughed and cried,

       Gm6   **A7**
I've had my fill, my share of losing.

   Dm   **Dm(maj7)**
And now, as tears sub - side,

     Dm7 G7   **C**
I find it all   so a - musing.

             C7   **F**
To think I did all that, and may I say,

      Fm
Not in a shy way.

    C   **G7**
Oh no, oh no, not me,

     F6 C
I did it my way.

Outro

          C   **C7**
For what is a man, what has he got?

     F
If not him - self, then he has naught.

    Dm7   **G7**
To say the things he truly feels

     Em   **Am**
And not the words of one who kneels,

    Dm7   **G7**
The record shows I took the blows,

    F6 C
And did it my way.

Over the Rainbow

from THE WIZARD OF OZ

Music by Harold Arlen
Lyric by E.Y. "Yip" Harburg

Melody:

When all the world is a hope-less jum-ble and the

Eb   Fm7   Eb6   Bb7   Ab   Ebmaj7   E°7   Bb7b9   Dm7

G7   Cm   Ab7   F9   Eb°7   Cm7   Gm   Eb7   Abmaj7

Gm7   G°7   Abm6   C7b9   F7   Fm6   C7

Intro | Eb | Fm7 | Eb6 | Bb7 |

Prelude

Eb   Ab
When all the world is a hopeless jumble

Ebmaj7   Fm7 Bb7
And the raindrops tumble all a - round,

Eb   E°7 Fm7   Bb7b9 Eb
Heav - en   opens a magic   lane.

Ab
When all the clouds darken up the skyway,

Ebmaj7   Dm7   G7
There's a rainbow highway to be found,

Cm   Ab7   F9   Fm7
Leading from your window - pane

Eb   Fm7
To a place behind the sun,

Eb   Eb°7   Fm7 Bb7
Just a step be - yond the rain.

Verse 1

E♭6   Cm7 Gm   E♭7
Some - where over the rain - bow

A♭ A♭maj7 A♭7 Gm7 G°7
Way up _____ high,

Fm7   A♭m6 E♭   C7♭9
There's a   land   that I heard of

F7   Fm7 B♭7 E♭
Once in a lull - a - by.

Verse 2

E♭6   Cm7 Gm   E♭7
Some - where over the rain - bow

A♭ A♭maj7 A♭7 Gm7 G°7
Skies are _____ blue,

Fm7 A♭m6 E♭   C7♭9 F7
And   the   dreams that you dare to dream

       Fm6 B♭7 E♭
Really do   come true.

Bridge

E♭
Some - day I'll wish upon a star

Fm7   **B♭7**   **E♭6**
And wake up where the clouds are far be - hind me.

B♭7   **E♭**
Where troubles melt like lemon drops,

E♭°7
A - way, above the chimney tops,

Fm6 **E♭°7 Fm7 B♭7**
That's where you'll find me.

Verse 3

E♭6 **Cm7** **Gm**   **E♭7**
Some - where over the rain - bow

A♭   **A♭maj7 A♭7 Gm7 G°7**
Blue - birds _____ fly.

Fm7 A♭m6 E♭   **C7**
Birds fly   over the rainbow,

F7   **B♭7**   **E♭**
Why then, oh why can't I?

Outro

Fm7 B♭7 E♭   **Fm7**
       If happy little bluebirds fly be - yond the rainbow,

B♭7   **E♭6**
Why, oh why can't I?

Night and Day

from THE GAY DIVORCE
Words and Music by
Cole Porter

Melody:

Like the beat, beat, beat of the tom-tom

B°7　Cm　C#°7　Bb　Ebm　E°7　Bb7　Eb

B7　E7　C7　F　Ab°7　Dbm6　Bmaj7　Ebmaj7

Eb6　Am7b5　Abm7　Gm7　Gb°7　Fm7　Gb　Bb7sus4

Intro　　|B°7　Cm　|C#°7　Bb　|Ebm　E°7　|Bb7　　　|

Prelude

    E°7　　　　　　　　Bb7
Like the beat, beat, beat of the tomtom

       Eb　　　Ebm
When the jungle shadows fall.

Bb7　　E°7　　Bb7　　　　　　Eb
Like the tick, tick, tock of the stately clock

    Ebm　　　　　Bb7
As it stands against the wall.

      B7　　　　　　　　E7
Like the drip, drip, drip of the raindrops,

      C7　　　　　　F
When the summer shower is through.

Ab°7　Eb　　　Ebm　Bb　　　Dbm6
So a voice with - in me keeps re - peating,

Eb　Bb7　Eb
You, you, you.

Verse 1

E♭   Bmaj7 B♭7   E♭maj7 E♭6
Night and day _____ you are the one.

  Bmaj7   B♭7   E♭maj7 E♭6
Only you ___ beneath the moon and under the sun.

   Am7♭5 A♭m7
Whether near to me or far,

  Gm7   G♭°7
It's no matter, darling, where you are,

 Fm7 B♭7sus4 B♭7   E♭
I think of you _____ night and day.

Verse 2

     Bmaj7 B♭7   E♭maj7 E♭6
Day and night _____ why is it so,

    Bmaj7   B♭7   E♭maj7 E♭6
That this long - ing for you follows wherever I go?

   Am7♭5 A♭m7
In the roaring traffic's boom,

  Gm7   G♭°7
In the silence of my lonely room,

 Fm7 B♭7sus4 B♭7   E♭
I think of you _____ night and day.

Outro

   G♭   E♭
Night and day under the hide of me

   G♭   E♭
There's an oh, such a hungry yearning burning in - side of me.

  Am7♭5 A♭m7   Gm7   G♭°7
And its torment won't be through 'till you let me spend my life

    B♭7sus4 B♭7 B♭7sus4 E♭ E♭6
Making love to you day and night, ___ night and day.

Piano Man

Words and Music
by Billy Joel

Melody:

> It's nine o' - clock on ___ a

Chord diagrams: C, G, F, Fmaj7, D7, Cmaj7, Em, Dm, D, Am, Am7, G7

Intro

C	G	F	C
Fmaj7	C	D7	G
C	G	F	C
F		C	F
Cmaj7	F Em Dm	C	F
Cmaj7	F Em Dm	

Verse 1

```
        C       G       F       C
It's nine o' - clock on a Saturday,

F           C           D     G
The regular crowd shuffles in.

          C       G       F
There's an old man __ sitting next to me
C       F                   C
Making love to his tonic and gin.
```

Interlude 1

C	G	F	C
F		C	
F		

Verse 2

          C   G   F   C
He says, "Son, can you play __ me a memory?

    F   C   D   G
I'm not really sure __ how it goes.

        C   G   F   C
But it's sad and it's sweet, and I knew it complete

      F   F   C
When I wore a young - er man's clothes."

Bridge 1

Am   Am7   D   F
La, la, la, ____ li, di, da.

Am   Am7   D
 La, la, ____ li, di, da,

   G   G7 C G7
Da, dum.

Chorus 1

C   G   F   C
Sing us a song, __ you're the piano man.

F   C   D   G
Sing us a song __ tonight.

          C   G   F   C
Well, we're all in the mood __ for a melody,

    F   F   C
And you've got us feeling al - right.

Interlude 2

| C | G | F | C |

| F | | C | F |

| Cmaj7 | F Em Dm | C | F |

| Cmaj7 | F Em Dm |

Verse 3

        C   G   F   C
Now, John at the bar __ is a friend of mine,

    F   C   D   G
He gets me my drinks for free.

          C   G   F   C
And he's quick with a joke __ or to light __ up your smoke

      F   F   C   F
But there's someplace that he'd __ rather be.

Verse 4

```
        C        G      F         C
He says, "Bill, I believe ___ this is killing me."
   F        C          D     G
As a smile ran a - way from his face.
        C        G          F          C
"Well, I'm sure that I could be a mov - ie star
   F        F             C
If I could get out ___ of this place."
```

Bridge 2

```
       Am      Am7      D    F
Oh, la, la, la, ____ di, di, da.
   Am      Am7     D
La, la, ____ di, di, da,
   G   G7   C   G7
Da, dum.
```

Verse 5

```
        C      G         F        C
Now, Paul is a real estate novelist
   F            C       D     G
Who never had time ___ for a wife.
           C          G        F            C
And he's talking with Da - vy, who's still in the Na - vy
   F                  C
And probably will be for life.
```

Interlude 3   *Repeat Interlude 1*

Verse 6

```
          C        G          F        C
And the wait - ress is practicing politics
   F         C              D     G
As the bus - 'nessmen slowly get stoned.
           C            G        F          C
Yes, they're sharing a drink ___ they call loneliness,
   F                       C
But it's better than drinkin' alone.
```

Piano Solo		Am		Am7		D		F	
		Am		Am7		D		F	
		Am		Am7		D			
		G				C		G7	

Chorus 2   *Repeat Chorus 1*

Interlude 4   *Repeat Interlude 2*

Verse 7

        C   G   F   C
It's a pretty good crowd __ for a Saturday

       F   C   D   G
And the manager gives me a smile.

         C   G   F   C
'Cause he knows that it's me they've been coming to see

       F   C   F
To for - get about life for a while.

Verse 8

        C   G   F   C
And the piano, it sounds like a carnival,

         F   C   D   G
And the mi - crophone smells like a beer.

       C   G   F   C
And they sit at the bar __ and put bread in my jar,

       F   C
And say, "Man, what are you doin' here?"

Bridge 3   *Repeat Bridge 1*

Chorus 3   *Repeat Chorus 1*

Outro		C		G		F		C		
		F				C		F		
		Cmaj7		F Em Dm		C		F		
		Cmaj7		F Em Dm		C			

Satin Doll

Words by Johnny Mercer and Billy Strayhorn
Music by Duke Ellington

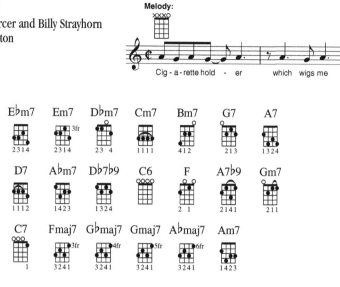

Melody:

Cig - a - rette hold - er   which wigs me

Dm7	Ebm7	Em7	Dbm7	Cm7	Bm7	G7	A7

Cm	D7	Abm7	Db7b9	C6	F	A7b9	Gm7

C7	Fmaj7	Gbmaj7	Gmaj7	Abmaj7	Am7

Intro

|Dm7 Ebm7 |Em7 Ebm7 |Dm7 Dbm7 |Cm7 Bm7 Cm7 Dbm7 |

Verse 1

Dm7   G7 Dm7 G7
Cigarette hold - er which wigs me,

Em7   A7
Over her shoul - der,

Em7 A7 Cm D7
She digs me. Out cattin'

Abm7 Db7b9 C6 F Em7 A7b9
That satin doll.

Verse 2

Dm7   G7 Dm7 G7
Baby, shall we ____ go out skippin'?

Em7   A7 Em7   A7
Careful, ami - go, you're flippin'.

Cm   D7 Abm7 Db7b9 C6
Speaks Latin, that satin doll.

Bridge

     Gm7   **C7**
She's nobody's fool,

     Gm7   **C7**   **Fmaj7 G♭maj7 Gmaj7 A♭maj7**
So I'm playing it cool as can be.

Am7   **D7**
I'll give it a whirl,

  Am7   **D7**   **G7 Dm7 D♭7♭9**
But I ain't for no girl catching me.   *Switcherooney.*

Verse 3

Dm7   **G7 Dm7** **G7**
Telephone num - bers,   well, you know,

Em7   **A7 Em7** **A7**
Doing my rhum - bas   with uno,

Cm **D7**   **A♭m7** **D♭7♭9 C6**
And that 'n'   my satin   doll.

Send in the Clowns

from the Musical
A LITTLE NIGHT MUSIC
Words and Music by
Stephen Sondheim

Melody:

Is-n't it rich?   Are we a pair?

D Dsus4 Dmaj7 Gmaj9 A G F#m C#m Bm

F# Bm7 Bm6 Gmaj7 F#7sus4 Em7b5 A6/9 A6 Dadd2

Intro

| D   Dsus4 |

Verse 1

D Dsus4 D   Dsus4   D
Isn't it rich? Are we a pair?

Dmaj7   Gmaj9
Me here at last on the ground, you in mid - air.

A   G
Send in the clowns.

Verse 2

Dsus4 D   Dsus4   D
Isn't it bliss? Don't you ap - prove?

Dmaj7   Gmaj9
One who keeps tearing around, one who can't move.

A   G   D
Where are the clowns? Send in the clowns.

Bridge

F#m   C#m   F#m
Just when I'd stopped opening doors,

C#m F#m   Bm
Finally knowing the one that I wanted was yours,

F#   Bm7   Bm6   Gmaj7 F#7sus4
Making my entrance a - gain with my usual   flair,

Em7♭5 A§ G   A   G A
Sure of my lines, no one is there.

Verse 3

Dsus4 D Dsus4 D
Isn't it rich? Isn't it queer,

      Dmaj7   Gmaj9
Losing my timing this late in my ca - reer?

        A6
And where are the clowns?

  G   A6
Quick, send in the clowns.

G   D Dsus4 D Dadd2
Don't bother, they're here.

September Song

from the Musical Play
KNICKERBOCKER HOLIDAY
Words by Maxwell Anderson
Music by Kurt Weill

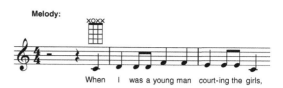

Melody:

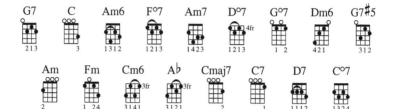

When I was a young man court-ing the girls,

G7   C   Am6   F°7   Am7   D°7   G°7   Dm6   G7#5

Am   Fm   Cm6   A♭   Cmaj7   C7   D7   C°7

Intro

| G7 | C Am6 | G7 | | |

Verse 1

     G7   F°7   Am7   Am6
When I was a young man courting the girls,

     G7   D°7   Am7
I played me a waiting game.

Am6 G7   F°7   Am7 G°7
If a   maid re - fused me with tossing curls,

   Dm6   G7#5   C   Am
I let the old earth take a couple of whirls,

        Fm   G7   Am Am6
While I plied her with tears in lieu of pearls.

       G7   F°7   Am   Am6
And as time came a - round she came my way,

       G7   C
As time came around she came.

Chorus 1

                     Cm6   **A♭**   **C**
Oh, it's a long, long while   from May to De - cember,

            Cmaj7 C7   D7
But the days   grow short

Fm   **G7**   **C**
When you reach Sep - tember.

                 Cm6   **A♭**   **C**
When the autumn weather   turns the leaves to flame,

           Cmaj7 C7   D7
One hasn't got time

         Fm   **G7** **C**
For the wait - ing game.

           Fm   **C°7**
Oh, the days dwindle down to a precious few,

          Fm   **C°7**
Sep - tember, No - vember.

C   **Cm6**   **A♭**   **C**
  And those few precious days   I'll spend with you,

       Cmaj7 C7   D7   **Fm**   **C**
These pre - cious days I'll spend with you.

Verse 2

             G7   **F°7**   **Am7 Am6**
When you meet with the young men early in spring,

     G7   **D°7**   **Am7**
They court you in song and rhyme.

Am6 G7   **F°7**   **Am7 G°7**
They   woo you with words and a clover ring,

    Dm6   **G7♯5**   **C**   **Am**
But if you ex - amine the goods they bring,

       Fm   **G7**   **Am**   **Am6**
They have little to offer but the songs they sing

     G7   **F°7**   **Am**   **Am6**
And a plentiful waste of time of day,

   G7   **C**
A plentiful waste of time.

Chorus 2   *Repeat Chorus 1*

Skylark

Words by Johnny Mercer
Music by Hoagy Carmichael

Melody:

Sky - lark, have you an - y-thing to say to me? _

Intro

| Gm Gm7 Gm6 Gm♯5 | F7sus4 Fm7 B♭7 |

Verse 1

Eb6 Bb7 Eb   Ab Eb Gm
Sky - lark, ___ have you anything to say to me?

Ab   Eb   Ab Eb
Won't you tell me where my love can be?

F7 Bb7   Eb
Is there a meadow in the mist,

     Ab Fm7 Bb7
Where someone's waiting to be kissed?

Verse 2

E♭6 B♭7 E♭   A♭   E♭   Gm
Sky - lark, ___ have you seen a valley green with spring,

A♭   E♭   A♭   E♭
Where my heart can go a journeying,

F7   B♭7   E♭
Over the shadows and the rain,

  B♭7   E♭
To a blossom covered lane?

Bridge

        A♭ A♭maj7 Fm7 E7 E♭7
And in your lone - ly   flight,

            A♭maj7 E♭°7 Fm7   D♭7 C7
Haven't you heard the music in   the   night?

      D°7   C7 Fm   D°7 D♭
Wonderful music, ___ faint as a "will o' wisp,"

Fm E♭7 A♭
Crazy as a loon,

G   A7   D7 G
Sad as a gypsy sere - nading the moon.

Outro

B♭7 E♭6 B♭7 E♭   A♭   E♭   Gm
Oh, Sky - lark, ___ I don't know if you can find these things,

A♭   E♭   A♭   E♭
But my heart is riding on your wings.

F7   B♭7   E♭   B♭7   E♭
So, if you see them any - where, won't you lead me there?

Some Day My Prince Will Come

Words by Larry Morey
Music by Frank Churchill

Melody:

(chord diagrams: F, Ab7, Gm, C7, A+, Bbo7, D7)

(chord diagrams: Bb+, E, Gm7, A7, Bo7, Ao7)

Intro | F | Ab7 | Gm | C7 |

Verse 1

F   A+   Bbo7   D7
Some day my prince will come,

Gm Bb+   C7
Some day I'll find my love,

         F   E   Gm7
And how thrilling that moment will be,

C7   F   E   Gm7 C7
  When the prince of my dreams comes to me.

F   A+   Bbo7 D7
He'll whisper, "I love you,"

Gm Bb+   C7
And steal a kiss or two.

          F   A7
Though he's far a - way

A+ Bb+   Bo7
I'll find my love some day,

       F   Ao7 Gm7   C7   F Ab7 Gm7 C7
Some day when my   dreams come true.

Verse 2

F   A+   B♭°7   D7
Some day I'll find my love,

Gm   B♭+   C7
Some - one to call my own,

        F   E   Gm7
And I'll know her the moment we meet,

C7   F   E   Gm7 C7
For my heart will start skipping a beat.

F   A+   B♭°7   D7
Some day we'll say and do

Gm   B♭+   C7
Things we've been longing to.

        F   A7
Though she's far a - way

A+ B♭+   B°7
I'll find my love some day,

      F   A°7 Gm7   C7   F
Some day when my   dreams come true.

Someone to Watch Over Me

from OH, KAY!

Music and Lyrics by
George Gershwin and Ira Gershwin

Melody:

There's a say - ing old says that love is blind,

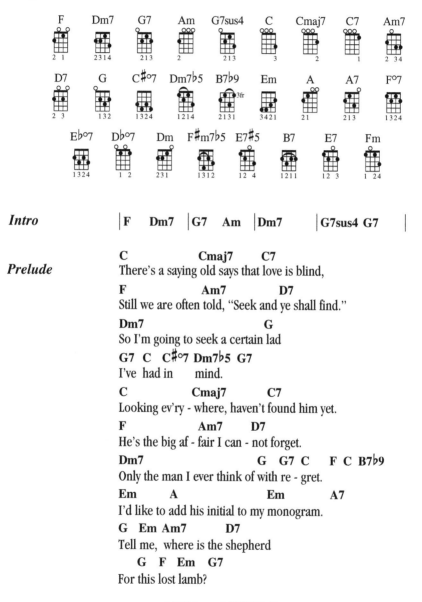

Intro |F   Dm7 |G7 Am |Dm7 |G7sus4 G7 |

Prelude

C   Cmaj7   C7
There's a saying old says that love is blind,

F   Am7   D7
Still we are often told, "Seek and ye shall find."

Dm7   G
So I'm going to seek a certain lad

G7 C C#°7 Dm7b5 G7
I've had in   mind.

C   Cmaj7   C7
Looking ev'ry - where, haven't found him yet.

F   Am7   D7
He's the big af - fair I can - not forget.

Dm7   G G7 C   F C B7b9
Only the man I ever think of with re - gret.

Em   A   Em   A7
I'd like to add his initial to my monogram.

G   Em Am7   D7
Tell me, where is the shepherd

     G   F Em G7
For this lost lamb?

Verse 1

```
C                    C7   F        F°7
There's a somebod - y I'm longing to see.

C        Eb°7 G7        Db°7
I hope that he    turns out to be

Dm      A7 Dm
Some - one who'll

F#m7b5  F  G7  C  E7#5  F  G7
Watch    o - ver me.
```

Verse 2

```
C     C7              F        F°7
I'm a little lamb who's lost in the wood.

C        Eb°7 G7        Db°7
I know I could always be good

Dm  A7 Dm
To one who'll

F#m7b5  F  G7  C  C7  F  G7
Watch    o - ver me.
```

Bridge

```
C            F
Although he may not be the man

   F°7  F          C
Some girls think of as handsome,

   B7        E7        A7  D7  G7
To my heart he carries the key.
```

Verse 3

```
C                 C7    F          F°7
Won't you tell him please to put on some speed,

C        Eb°7 G7        Db°7
Follow my lead,  oh, how I need

Dm      A7 Dm
Some - one to

F#m7b5  F  G7  C  C7  F  Fm  C
Watch    o - ver me.
```

Spanish Eyes

Words by Charles Singleton and Eddie Snyder
Music by Bert Kaempfert

Melody:

Blue _____ Span-ish eyes,

G   D7   G7   C   Cm   Ab

Intro   ‖: G | :‖

Verse 1

G
Blue Spanish eyes,

                        D7
Teardrops are falling from your Spanish eyes.

Please, please don't cry.

                 G
This is just adios and not good - bye.

Chorus 1

G
Soon I'll return,

           G7   **C**
Bringing you all the love your heart can hold.

Cm   **G**
Please say Si - si.

D7   **G**
Say you and your Spanish eyes will wait for me.

UKULELE CHORD SONGBOOK

	G
Verse 2	Blue Spanish eyes,

                                        D7
                        Prettiest eyes in all of Mexi - co.

                        True Spanish eyes,

                                                      G
                        Please smile for me once more before I go.

Chorus 2   *Repeat Chorus 1*

                        A♭
Outro   Spanish eyes, wait for me,

                                G A♭ G
                        Say Si - si!

Speak Softly Love (Love Theme)

from the Paramount Picture THE GODFATHER
Words by Larry Kusik
Music by Nino Rota

Melody:

Speak soft - ly, love, and hold me

Intro |Am |Dm |E |Am |

Verse 1
          Am   Dm   Am
Speak softly, love, and hold me warm against your heart.

                   Am   Dm
I feel your words, the tender, trembling moments start.

              Am
We're in a world our very own,

          Am   E7sus4 E7 Am
Sharing a love that only few have ever known.

Bridge 1

        G7 G7   **C**
Wine colored days warmed by the sun,

        Bbmaj7 Bm7b5   **E7sus4 E**
Deep velvet nights   when we are one.

Verse 2

             Am   **Dm**   **Am**
Speak softly, love, so no one hears us but the sky.

             Am   **Dm**
The vows of love we make will live until we die.

               Am
My life is yours and all be - cause

        Am   **E7sus4 E7 Am**   **F7**
You came in - to my world with love   so softly, love.

Instrumental |**Bbm Ebm** |**Bbm** | |**Ebm** |

                       |**Bbm** |**F7sus4 F7** |**Bbm** |

Bridge 2

        Ab7   **Db**
Wine colored days warmed by the sun,

        Bmaj7 Cm7b5   **F**
Deep velvet nights   when we are one.

Verse 3

      N.C.   **Bm**   **Em**   **Bm**
  Speak softly, love, so no one hears us but the sky.

             Bm   **Em**
The vows of love we make will live until we die.

               Bm
My life is yours and all be - cause

        Bm   **F#7sus4 F#7**   **Bm Em F#7 Bm**
You came in - to my world with love   so softly, love.

Stardust

Words by Mitchell Parish
Music by Hoagy Carmichael

Melody:

And now the pur-ple dusk of   twi-light time

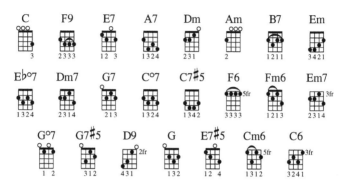

Verse 1

    C   F9
And now the purple dusk of twilight time

E7   A7
Steals across the meadows of my heart.

Dm   C   Am
High up in the sky the little stars climb,

B7   Em E♭°7 Dm7 G7
Always reminding me that we're a - part.

Verse 2

    C   F9
You wandered down the lane and far away,

E7   A7
Leaving me a song that will not die.

Dm   C   C°7
Love is now the stardust of yesterday,

G7   C
The music of the years gone by.

Chorus 1

C7♯5 F6   Fm6
Some - times I wonder why I spend the lonely night

Dreaming of a song.

C   Em7   A7
The melody haunts my rever - ie,

Dm7   A7   Dm7
And I am once again with you,

G7 G°7 G7
When our love was new,

G7♯5 C
And each kiss an inspi - ration.

D9
But that was long ago,

                   G7   Dm7   G7 G°7
Now my consolation is in the stardust of a song.

Chorus 2

G7 C7♯5 F6   Fm6
  Be - side a garden wall, when stars are bright, you are in my arms.

C   Em7   A7
The nightingale tells his fairy tale

Dm7   A7   Dm7
  Of para - dise, where roses grew.

Fm6   C   G Am C B7
  Tho' I dream in vain, in my heart it will re - main

E7 E7♯5 F6   A7 E♭°7
  My   stardust melo - dy,

G7   G7   C Cm6 C6
  The memo - ry of love's re - frain.

Stormy Weather
(Keeps Rainin' All the Time)

Lyric by Ted Koehler
Music by Harold Arlen

Melody:

Don't know why ___ there's no sun up in the sky,

G   G#°7   Am7   D9   D7#5   C   Bb7b5   A7   D7b9

D7   Cm6   Am7b5   Cm9   G9   A9   D   Em7   F°7

Intro

‖: G   G#°7 | Am7   D9 :‖

Verse 1

    G   G#°7   Am7   D9
Don't know why ___ there's no sun up in the sky,
    G Am7   G
Stormy weather, since my man and I ain't to - gether,
Am7   D7#5 G   Am7   D9
Keeps rainin' all ___ the time.

Verse 2

    G   G#°7   Am7   D9
Life is bare, ___ gloom and mis'ry ev'ry - where,
    G Am7   G
Stormy weather, just can't get my poor self to - gether.
Am7   D7#5 G   G#°7
I'm weary all ___ the time, the time,
Am7   D7#5 G   Am7   G
So weary all ___ the time.

Bridge 1

  C   G
When he went away the blues walked in and met me.
  C   G
If he stays away old rockin' chair will get me.
  C   G
All I do is pray the Lord a - bove will let me
     Bb7b5   A7 D7b9
Walk in the sun once   more.

Verse 3

D7   G G#°7   Am7   D9
Can't go on, ____ ev'ry - thing I had is gone,

      G   Am7   G
Stormy weather, since my man and I ain't to - gether,

Am7   D7#5   G
Keeps rainin' all ____ the time,

Am7   D7#5   G
Keeps rainin' all ____ the time.

Bridge 2

Cm6   Am7♭5   Cm9
I walk a - round, heavy hearted and sad.

G9
Night comes around and I'm still feeling bad.

A9
Rain pourin' down, blindin' ev'ry hope I had.

     D   Em7   F°7   D7
This pitterin', patterin', beatin', an' splatterin' drives me mad.

G9   A9
Love, love, love, love,

Am7   D7
This misery is just too much for me.

Verse 4

D7   G G#°7   Am7   D9
Can't go on, ____ ev'ry - thing I had is gone,

      G   Am7   G
Stormy weather, since my man and I ain't to - gether,

Am7   D7#5   G
Keeps rainin' all ____ the time,

Am7   D7#5   G
Keeps rainin' all ____ the time.

Summertime
from PORGY AND BESS ®
Music and Lyrics by George Gershwin,
Du Bose and Dorothy Heyward and
Ira Gershwin

Sum - mer - time _____ an' the liv - in' is

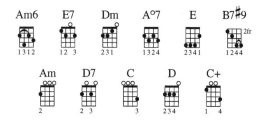

Intro | Am6 E7 | Am6 E7 |

Verse 1

Am6 E7   Am6 E7
Summer - time

Am6   E7   Am6 E7
An' the livin' is eas - y.

Am6 E7   Dm
Fish are jumpin'

A°7 E B7#9
An' the cotton is   high.

E   Am6   E7
Oh, your daddy's rich,

Am6   E7   Am6 E7
An' your ma is good look - in'.

Am D7   C   Am
So hush, little baby,

D   Dm Am C+ Am6 C+
Don't you cry.

Verse 2

D7 C+   Am6   E7
One of these mornin's

Am6   E7   Am6 E7
You goin' to rise up sing - in'.

Am6 E7   Dm
Then you'll spread your wings

A°7 E   B7#9
An' you'll take the   sky.

E   Am6   E7
But 'til that mornin'

Am6   E7   Am6 E7
There's a nothin' can harm you,

Am D7   C   Am
With Daddy an' Mammy

D   Dm Am E7 Am6
Stand - in'   by.

Tears in Heaven

Words and Music by
Eric Clapton and Will Jennings

Melody:

Would you know my name

D	A	Bm	Bm7	G	Asus4	A7	F♯	D7
222	21	3111	1111	132	23	1	3121	3 2

B7	B7sus4	Em	Em7	F	C	Dm	Am
1211	1311	3421	3121	2 1	3	231	1

Intro |D   A Bm | Bm7 |G Asus4 A |D |

Verse 1

```
D            A      Bm    Bm7
Would you know my name
G   D              A   D   A7
If I saw you in heav - en?
D        A     Bm    Bm7
Would it be the same
G   D              A   D   A7
If I saw you in heav - en?
```

Chorus 1

```
Bm                 F♯
I must be strong
D7          B7
And carry on,
B7sus4 B7     Em
'Cause   I   know
Em7        Asus4
I don't belong
            D   A   Bm   Bm7  G   Asus4  A   D
Here in heav - en.
```

Verse 2

D   A   Bm   Bm7
Would you hold my hand

G D   A   D A7
If I saw you in heav - en?

D   A   Bm   Bm7
Would ya help me stand

G D   A   D A7
If I saw you in heav - en?

Chorus 2

Bm   F♯
I'll find my way

D7   B7
Through night and day

B7sus4 B7   Em
'Cause   I know

Em7   Asus4
I just can't stay

            D A Bm   Bm7 G Asus4 A D
Here in heav - en.

Bridge

F   C   Dm
Time can bring ya down,

          G   C G Am G C
Time can bend your knees.

F   C   Dm
Time can break your heart,

        G   C
Have ya beggin' please,

G   A D A7
Beggin' please.

Interlude   *Repeat Verse 2 (Instrumental)*

Chorus 3

Bm   F#
Beyond the door

D7   B7
There's peace, I'm sure,

B7sus4 B7 Em
And I know

   Em7 Asus4
There'll be no more

      D A Bm Bm7 G Asus4 A D
Tears in heav - en.

Verse 3   *Repeat Verse 1*

Chorus 4

Bm   F#
I must be strong

D7   B7
And carry on,

B7sus4 B7 Em
'Cause I know

Em7 Asus4
I don't belong

    D A Bm
Here in heav - en.

Bm7 Em
 'Cause I know

Em7 Asus4
I don't belong

    D A Bm Bm7 G Asus4 A D
Here in heav - en.

Unforgettable

Words and Music by
Irving Gordon

Melody:

Un - for - get-ta - ble, ___ that's what you are.

G A7 D9 Am7 D7♭9 G°7 C A9 Em7 Cm

F Fm Em7♭5 D♭9 D7 G7 Dm7 D♭7 C6

Intro | G | | A7 | D9   Am7 D7♭9 |

Verse 1
G   G°7
Unforgettable, that's what you are.

C   A9 Em7 Cm A9
Unforgettable, though near or far.

F   Fm
Like a song of love that clings to me,

C   Em7♭5   A7
How the thought of you does things to me.

D9   D♭9 D9
Never before has   someone been more…

Verse 2
G   G°7
Unforgettable, in ev'ry way,

C   A9 Em7 Cm A9
And forevermore, that's how you'll stay.

F   Fm
That's why, darling, it's incredible,

C   Em7♭5 A7
That some - one so   unforgettable

D7   G7   C Dm7 D♭7 C6
Thinks that I am unforgettable too.

They Can't Take That Away from Me

Music and Lyrics by
George Gershwin and Ira Gershwin

Melody:

Our ro - mance won't end on a sor - row - ful

Fm7 F°7 Bb7sus4 Bb7 Eb E°7 Eb6 B7 Am7

D7 G6 Gmaj7 Gm Ab C+ C7 Bb Db°7

F7 Gb°7 Bb7#5 Gm7b5 Gm7 D9 Em7b5 Abmaj7 Fm7b5

Intro

| Fm7 F°7 Bb7sus4 Bb7 |

Verse 1

Eb   E°7   Fm7   Bb7   Eb6
Our ro - mance won't end on a sorrowful note,

B7   Bb7   Eb
Though by to - morrow you're gone.

        E°7   Fm7   Bb7   Eb
The song is ended, but as the songwriter wrote,

    Am7   D7   G6
The melody lingers on.

Am7   D7   Gmaj7
They may take you from me,

    Am7   D7   Gm
I'll miss your fond ca - ress.

    Ab   C+ C7   E°7
But though they take you from me,

Fm7 Bb Db°7 F7   Bb7
I'll   still pos - sess…

Verse 2

A♭   E♭ Fm7
The way you wear your hat,

E♭   G♭°7 Fm7 B♭7sus4 B♭7
The way you sip your tea,

Fm7   A♭ E♭ B♭7#5
The mem'ry of all that,

Gm7♭5 A♭ Fm7 C7 F7
No, no, they can't take that a - way from me!

Verse 3

A♭   E♭ Fm7
The way your smile just beams,

E♭   G♭°7 Fm7 B♭7sus4 B♭7
The way you sing off key,

Fm7   A♭   E♭ B♭7#5
The way you haunt my dreams,

Gm7♭5 A♭ Fm7 B♭7sus4 B♭7 E♭6
No, no, they can't take that a - way from me!

Bridge

    Gm7 C7 Gm7 C7
We may never, never meet a - gain

D9 Gm7   Em7♭5 Am7 D7
On the bumpy road ___ to love.

   Gm7 C7
Still I'll always, always

Gm7 C7 F7 B♭7
Keep the mem'ry of…

Verse 4

A♭   A♭maj7 Fm7 E♭ Fm7
The way you hold your knife,

E♭   G♭°7   Fm7 B♭7sus4 B♭7
The way we danced 'till three,

    A♭ Gm7♭5
The way you changed my life.

   A♭ Fm7 B♭7sus4 B♭7 E♭6
No, no, they can't take that a - way from me!

Fm7♭5 E♭ A♭ E♭
No, they can't take that

A♭ Fm7 B♭ E♭6
A - way from me!

A Time for Us (Love Theme)
from the Paramount Picture ROMEO AND JULIET
Words by Larry Kusik and Eddie Snyder
Music by Nino Rota

Melody:

A time _ for us _

Am   F   G   Em   C   Dm   E   B♭   A

Intro | Am | F | G | Am |

Verse 1
                   Em   **F**
A time for us someday there'll be

                        C   **Dm**   **Am**
When chains are torn by courage born of a love that's free.

                   Em   **F**   **Dm**   **E**
A time when dreams so long de - nied can flour - ish

         Am   **Em** **Am**
As we unveil the love we now must hide.

Bridge 1
        C   **G** **Dm** **Am**
A time for us at last to see

        B♭   **F**   **Em**   **Am**
A life worth - while for you and me.

Verse 2

         Em   F
And with our love through tears and thorns

       C   Dm   Am
We will en - dure as we pass surely through ev'ry storm.

      Em   F   Dm E
A time for us someday there'll be a new world,

 Am   Em Am
A world of shining hope for you and me.

Bridge 2   *Repeat Bridge 1*

Verse 3

         Em   F
And with our love through tears and thorns

       C   Dm   Am
We will en - dure as we pass surely through ev'ry storm.

      Em   F   Dm E
A time for us someday there'll be a new world,

 Am   Em Am Em A
A world of shining hope for you and me.

Top of the World

Words and Music by
John Bettis and Richard Carpenter

Melody:

Such a feel - in's com - in' o - ver me. ___

Chords: Bm6 D E7 A Bm E C#m Bm7 F#7 Bm7b5 Esus4 G

Intro

Bm6 D E7	A		D A Bm A	D		
		A	E7	A		
		D	A D	A D	
A E D E	

Verse 1

```
         A        E      D    A
Such a feel in's comin' o - ver me.
              C#m              Bm      E7   A
There is wonder in most ev'rything ___ I ___ see.
Bm7 A  D            E7
Not   a  cloud in the sky,
              C#m        F#7
Got the sun in my eyes
          Bm              Bm7b5      Esus4 E D E
And I   won't be surprised ___ if it's a dream.
```

Verse 2

```
         A        E           D    A
Ev'rything I want the world ___ to be
              C#m           Bm    E7     A
Is now coming true, es - pecially ___ for ___ me.
Bm7 A  D            E7
And   the reason is clear,
              C#m        F#7
It's be - cause you are here.
          Bm              Bm7b5           E
You're the nearest thing to heaven that I've ___ seen.
```

Chorus 1

     D E A   **D A**
I'm on the   top of the world,

     D   **G D**
Lookin'   down on crea - tion

     A   **Bm7**   **A**
And the only explana - tion I can ___ find

Bm7 A D   **E**
Is   the love that I've found

     A   **D**
Ever since you've been around.

         A   **Bm E**   **A**
Your love's put me at the top of the world.

Interlude

|A   D |A   D |A   D |A E D E |

Verse 3

A   **E**   **D**   **A**
Something in the wind has learned ___ my name.

   C#m   **Bm**   **E7**   **A**
And it's tellin' me that things are not ___ the ___ same.

Bm7 A D   **E7**
In   the leaves on the trees

   C#m   **F#7**
And the touch of the breeze,

     Bm7   **Bm7♭5**   **Esus4 E D E**
There's a pleasin' sense of hap - piness for me.

Verse 4

A   **E**   **D**   **A**
There is only one wish on ___ my mind.

   C#m   **Bm**   **E7**   **A**
When this day is through I hope that I ___ will ___ find

Bm7 A D   **E7**
That   to - morrow will be

   C#m   **F#7**
Just the same for you and me.

   Bm7   **Bm7♭5**   **E**
All I need will be mine if you are ___ here.

Chorus 2

Repeat Chorus 1

Outro

|A   D |A   D |A   D |A E A   ‖

Unchained Melody
from the Motion Picture UNCHAINED

Lyric by Hy Zaret
Music by Alex North

C   Am   F   G   Em   C7   E♭   Fm

Verse 1

      C   Am   F
Whoa, my ___ love, my ___ darlin',

    G   C   Am   G
I've hungered for your ___ touch, a long lonely time.

     C   Am   F
And time goes ___ by so ___ slowly

    G   C
And time can do so ___ much.

     Am   G
Are ___ you still mine?

     C   G Am   Em
I ___ need your love.   I need ___ your love.

     F   G   C C7
God   speed your love to me.

Bridge

    F   G   F   E♭
Lonely rivers flow to the sea, to the sea,

    F   G   C
To the open arms of the sea, yeah.

    F   G   F   E♭
Lonely rivers sigh, "Wait for me, wait for me.

    F   G   C
I'll be comin' home, wait for me."

Verse 2

    C   Am   F
Whoa, my ___ love, my ___ darlin',

    G   C   Am   G
I've hungered, hungered for your ___ touch, a long lonely time.

     C   Am   F
And time goes ___ by so ___ slowly

     G   C
And time can do so ___ much.

    Am   G
Are ___ you still mine?

     C   G   Am   Em
I ___ need your ___ love. I ___ need ___ your love.

      F   G   C Am F Fm C
God speed your love to me.

We've Only Just Begun

Words and Music by
Roger Nichols and Paul Williams

Melody:

We've on - ly just be-gun ___

Chord diagrams:
A   Dmaj7   C#m7   F#m7   Bm7   E7sus4   E7
21 1113   12 3   1314   412   12 3   12 3

Amaj7   E   F#   Bmaj7   Bb   Ebmaj7 (3fr)   C# (4fr)
1333   2341 3121   4321   3211   1113   3211

Intro
| A | Dmaj7 | A | Dmaj7 |

Verse 1

    A   Dmaj7 C#m7
  We've only just be - gun to live,

  F#m7   Bm7
  White lace and ___ promises,

  F#m7   Bm7   E7sus4 E7
  A kiss for luck and we're on our way.

Verse 2

    A   Dmaj7 C#m7
  Before the rising sun we _____ fly.

  F#m7 Bm7
  So many roads to choose,

  F#m7   Bm7   E7sus4
  We start out walking and learn to run.

            Amaj7 Dmaj7 Amaj7 Dmaj7 E
  (And, yes, we've just be - gun.)

Bridge 1

F#　　Bmaj7　　F#　　Bmaj7
Sharing ho - rizons that are new to us,

F#　　　　Bmaj7　　F# Bmaj7
Watching the signs ___ along the way.

Bb　　Ebmaj7　　Bb　　Ebmaj7
Talking it over, just the two of us,

Bb　　　　Ebmaj7　　E7sus4　E7
Working to - gether day to day, to - gether.

Verse 3

A　　　　　　Dmaj7　　C#m7
And when the evening comes we smile,

F#m7　　Bm7
So much of life ahead,

F#m7　　　　　　　　　Bm7　　　E7sus4
We'll find a place where there's room to grow.

　　　　　　　　　　Amaj7 Dmaj7 Amaj7 Dmaj7 E
(And, yes, we've just be - gun.)

Bridge 2

F#　　Bmaj7　　F#　　Bmaj7
Sharing ho - rizons that are new to us,

F#　　　　Bmaj7　　F# Bmaj7
Watching the signs ___ along the way.

Bb　　Ebmaj7　　Bb　　Ebmaj7
Talking it over, just the two of us,

Bb　　　　Ebmaj7　　E7sus4 E7　　N.C.
Working to - gether day to day, to - gether, together.

Verse 4

A　　　　　　Dmaj7　　C#m7
And when the evening comes we smile,

F#m7　　Bm7
So much of life ahead,

F#m7　　　　　　　　　Bm7　　　E7sus4
We'll find a place where there's room to grow.

　　　　　　　　　　Amaj7 Dmaj7 Amaj7 Dmaj7 C#
And, yes, we've just be - gun.

What a Wonderful World

Words and Music by
George David Weiss and Bob Thiele

Intro
| F   Gm | F   Gm |

Verse 1

F   Am   B♭   Am
I see trees of green,   red roses, too.

Gm   F   A7   Dm
I see them bloom   for me and you,

D♭   Gm7   C7   F   F+ B♭maj7 C7
And I think to myself,   "What a wonderful world."

Verse 2

F   Am   B♭   Am
I see skies of blue and clouds of white,

Gm7   F   A7   Dm
The bright blessed day, the dark sacred night,

D♭   Gm7   C7   F   B♭
And I think to myself,   "What a wonderful world."

Bridge

F   C7   F
The colors of the rainbow, so pretty in the sky,

C7   F
Are also on the faces of people goin' by.

Dm   C   Dm   C
I see friends shakin' hands, sayin', "How do you do!"

Dm   F#°7   Gm7 F#°7 C
They're really sayin', "I   love   you."

Verse 3

C7   F   Am Bb   Am
I hear babies cry, I watch them grow;

Gm   F   A7   Dm
They'll learn much more than I'll ever know,

Db   Gm7   C7   F   Am7b5 D7
And I think to myself,   "What a wonderful world."

Gm7   C7b9   F   Gm7 F
Yes, I think to myself, "What a wonderful world."

What Is This Thing Called Love?

Words and Music by
Cole Porter

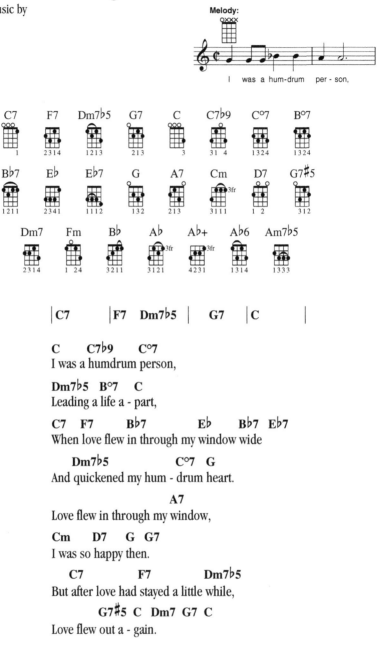

Intro |C7 |F7 Dm7♭5 | G7 |C |

Verse 1

C   C7♭9   C°7
I was a humdrum person,

Dm7♭5 B°7 C
Leading a life a - part,

C7 F7   B♭7   E♭   B♭7 E♭7
When love flew in through my window wide

  Dm7♭5   C°7 G
And quickened my hum - drum heart.

             A7
Love flew in through my window,

Cm   D7   G G7
I was so happy then.

    C7   F7   Dm7♭5
But after love had stayed a little while,

  G7♯5 C Dm7 G7 C
Love flew out a - gain.

Chorus 1

C7   Dm7♭5
What is this thing called love?

 G7 G7♯5 C
This funny thing called love?

C7   C7♭9 Dm7♭5
Just who can solve its myster - y?

 G7   G7♯5 C C7 Fm C
Why should it make a fool of me?

Cm F7   B♭
I saw you there one wonderful day.

 A♭ A♭+ A♭6   G Am7♭5
You took my heart ___ and threw it a - way.

G7 N.C.   C   C7♭9   Dm7♭5
 That's why I ask the Lord in heaven a - bove,

 G7   G7♯5 C Dm7♭5 C
What is this thing called love?

Verse 2

 C   C7♭9 C°7
You gave me days of sunshine,

Dm7♭5 B°7 C
You gave me nights of cheer,

C7 F7 B♭7 E♭ B♭7
You made my life an en - chanted dream,

E♭7 Dm7♭5   F♯°7 G
 'Till somebody else came near.

        A7
Somebody else came near you,

Cm D7 G
I felt the winter's chill.

G7 C7   F7   Dm7♭5
 And now I sit and wonder night and day

 G7♯5 C Dm7 G7 C
Why I love you still.

Chorus 2   *Repeat Chorus 1*

When I Fall in Love

Words by Edward Heyman
Music by Victor Young

Melody:

When I fall in love

D E7 Em7 A7sus4 A7 Gadd2 B7#5 B7 G°7

Am B7b9 Em A G Gm6 G9 Bb9 D6

Intro | D | E7 | Em7 | A7sus4 A7 |

Verse 1
D   Em7 Gadd2
When I fall in love

D   A7sus4 A7
It will be for - ever,

D   B7#5 B7 Em7
Or I'll never fall   in   love.

G°7 D   G°7
    In a restless world like this is,

D   Am   B7
Love is ended be - fore it's be - gun,

Em7   B7b9
And too many moonlight kisses

Em   Em7   A   A7
Seem to cool in the warmth of the sun.

Verse 2

D   Em7 Gadd2
When I give my heart

D   A7sus4 A7
It will be com - pletely,

D   B7#5 B7 Em7
Or I'll never give my heart.

G°7   D   G
And the moment I can feel

          B7   Em7
That you feel that way too

Gm6 D   Em7
Is   when I fall in love

A7 D G9 B♭9 D D6
With you.

When You Wish Upon a Star

Words by Ned Washington
Music by Leigh Harline

Melody:

When a star is born,

C   Eb°7   Dm   F   G9   G7b9   G7   Am   E7

Cmaj7   D7   G°7   G7#5   A7   Dm7   Fadd2   Fm6   Em

Intro
| C   Eb°7 | Dm | F   G9   G7b9 | C   G7 |

Prelude
C   G7   C   G7
When a star is born,

C   G7   C   G9   G7b9
They pos - sess a gift or two.

Am   E7   Am
One of them is this:

           Cmaj7   D7
They have the power ___ to make

  G°7   G7   G7#5
A wish come true.

Verse 1
C   A7   Dm   Dm7
When you wish up - on a star,

G7   Eb°7   C
Makes no diff'rence who you are,

  Eb°7   Dm   F
Any - thing your heart de - sires

   Fadd2   G7   Cmaj7
Will come   to   you.

Verse 2

C   A7   Dm   Dm7
If your heart is in your dream,

G7   E♭°7   C
No request is too ex - treme,

E♭°7   Dm F
When you wish up - on a star

Fadd2 G7 C
As dream - ers do.

Bridge

Fm6 Em Cmaj7
Fate   is   kind,

Dm G°7 G7 E♭°7   C
She   brings to   those who love,

Am   D7   Fm6 G7
The sweet ful - fillment of their secret long - ing.

Verse 3

C   A7   Dm Dm7
Like a bolt out of the blue,

G7   E♭°7 C
Fate steps in and sees you thru.

E♭°7   Dm F
When you wish up - on a star

Fadd2 G7   C
Your dream comes true.

Yesterday

Words and Music by John Lennon
and Paul McCartney

Melody:

Yes-ter-day, _   all my trou-bles seemed so   far   a - way. _

F   Em   A7   Dm   Dm7   B♭

C7   Fmaj7   G   C   Gm6

Intro

| F | | |

Verse 1

 F **Em**
Yesterday,

  A7   **Dm** **Dm7**
All my troubles seemed so far away.

B♭ **C7**   **F** **Fmaj7**
Now it looks as though they're here to stay.

 Dm **G** **B♭** **F**
Oh, I believe __ in yes - terday.

Verse 2

 F **Em**
Suddenly,

  A7   **Dm** **Dm7**
I'm not half the man I used to be.

B♭   **C7**   **F**   **Fmaj7**
There's a shad - ow hanging over me,

 Dm **G** **B♭** **F**
Oh, yesterday __ came sud - denly.

Bridge 1

       Em A7 Dm C B♭
Why she had to go

           Gm6   C7   F
I don't know, she wouldn't say.

       Em A7 Dm   C   B♭
I   said some - thing wrong.

          Gm6   C7   F
Now I ___ long for yester - day.

Verse 3

       F   Em
Yesterday,

            A7   Dm   Dm7
Love was such an easy game to play.

B♭   C7   F   Fmaj7
 Now I need a place to hide away.

    Dm   G   B♭ F
Oh, I believe ___ in yes - terday.

Bridge 2   *Repeat Bridge 1*

Verse 4

       F   Em
Yesterday,

            A7   Dm   Dm7
Love was such an easy game to play.

B♭   C7   F   Fmaj7
 Now I need a place to hide away.

    Dm   G   B♭ F
Oh, I believe ___ in yes - terday.

    G B♭ F
Mm.

You Are So Beautiful

Words and Music by Billy Preston
and Bruce Fisher

You are so ___ beau-ti - ful ___

Ab Ab7 Fm7 Db Abmaj7 Dbmaj7 Gb9

Ebm C7 C+ Fm Fm(maj7) Bb9 Bb7#11

Intro ‖: Ab Ab7 | Fm7 Db :‖

Verse 1

Ab   Abmaj7 Ab7   Dbmaj7   Gb9
You are _____ so ___ beautiful

Ab   Ab7
To me.

Ab Abmaj7 Ab7   Dbmaj7   Gb9
You are _____ so ___ beautiful

Ab   Abmaj7
To me.

        Ebm   Ab7
Can't you see?

Dbmaj7   C7   C+ C7
You're ev'rything I hope for.

Fm   Fm(maj7) Fm7 Bb9
You're ___ ev'ry - thing I need.

Ab   Abmaj7 Ab7 Dbmaj7   Gb9
You are _____ so ____ beautiful

Ab   Abmaj7
To me.

Verse 2

A♭   A♭maj7 A♭7 D♭maj7   G♭9
You are _____ so ___ beautiful

A♭   A♭7
To me.

A♭ A♭maj7 A♭7 D♭maj7   G♭9
You are _____ so ___ beautiful

A♭   A♭maj7
To me.

     E♭m   A♭7
Can't you see?

D♭maj7   C7   C+ C7
You're ev'rything I hope for.

Fm   B♭7♯11
  Ev'rything I need.

A♭   A♭maj7 A♭7 D♭maj7   G♭9
You are _____ so ___ beautiful

A♭ A♭maj7 A♭7 D♭maj7 G♭9 A♭
To ___ me.

You Are the Sunshine of My Life

Words and Music by
Stevie Wonder

Melody:

You are the sun - shine of __ my __ life, __

Bmaj9   F#7#5   B   F#7   D#m7   G7b9   C#m7   E

Bmaj7   D#7   D#+   D#   G#maj7   C#maj7   G#m7   C#7

G7   C   Em7   A7b9   Dm7   F

Intro   ‖: Bmaj9 | | F#7#5 | :‖

Chorus 1

B   F#7   D#m7 G7b9
You are the sun - shine of my life,

C#m7   F#7   B C#m7 F#7
That's why I'll al - ways be around.

B   F#7   D#m7 G7b9
You are the ap - ple of my eye.

C#m7   E   B C#m7 F#7
Forever you'll __ stay in my heart.

Verse 1

B   F#7   E   Bmaj7   F#7 E
I feel like this ___ is the __ be - ginning,

Bmaj7   E   D#7 D#m7 D#+ D#
'Though I've loved you for a million years.

G#maj7 C#maj7   D#   G#m7
And if I thought our love ___ was ___ ending,

      C#7   F#7
I'd find ___ myself drowning in my own tears.

Whoa, whoa.

Chorus 2

B   F#7   D#m7 G7b9
You are the sun - shine of my life,

C#m7   F#7   B C#m7 F#7
That's why I'll al - ways stay around.

B   F#7   D#m7 G7b9
You are the ap - ple of my eye.

C#m7   E   B C#m7 F#7
Forever you __ stay in my heart.

Verse 2

B   F#7   E Bmaj7   F#7 E
You must have known ___ that I __ was ___ lonely,

Bmaj7   E   D#7 D#m7 D#+ D#
Because you came __ to my rescue.

G#maj7   C#maj7   D#   G#m7
And I know that his must ___ be ___ heaven.

             C#7   F#7
How could so ___ much love be inside of you?

G7
Whoa,

Chorus 3

    C   G7   Em7 A7b9
‖: You are the sun - shine of my life,

Dm7   G7   C Dm7 G7
That's why I'll al - ways stay around.

C   G7   Em7 A7b9
You are the ap - ple of my eye.

Dm7   F   C Dm7 G7
Forever you __ stay in my heart.   :‖ *Repeat and fade*

You Raise Me Up

Words and Music by
Brendan Graham and
Rolf Lovland

Melody:

When I am down   and, oh, _ my soul's so wear-y, ___

D   G   Asus4   A7sus4   Dsus4   A7   Bm   A   E   Esus4

123   132   12   2   123   213   3111   21   2341   2341

B   Bsus4   C#m7   Asus2   Dm   B♭   F   C   C7   Csus4

3211   3411   12 3   2 3   231   3211   2 1   3   1   13

Intro

D			G	Asus4
G		D G D	G D	A7sus4
D	

Verse

    D   Dsus4   D
When I am down and, oh, my soul's so weary,

                    G   Asus4
When troubles come and my heart burdened be,

         G   D
Then I am still and wait here in the silence

    G   D   A7   D
Until you come and sit a while with me.

Chorus 1

              Bm   G   D
You raise me up so I can stand on mountains.

    A   Bm G   D
You raise me up to walk on stormy seas.

    A   D   G   D
I am strong when I am on your shoulders.

    G   D   A7   D
You raise me up to more than I can be.

Interlude

```
|E   Esus4 |E        |     A  |E   B   |
|A         |E   A    |E  Bsus4 |E       |
```

Chorus 2

     C#m7 A   E
You raise me up so I can stand on mountains.

B   C#m7 A   E
You raise me up to walk on stormy seas.

B E
I am strong when I am on your shoulders.

Asus2   E Bsus4   E A E
You raise me up to more than I can ___ be.

Chorus 3

N.C.   Dm B♭   F
You raise me up so I can stand on mountains.

C   Dm B♭   F
You raise me up to walk on stormy seas.

C F   B♭   F
I am strong when I am on your shoulders.

B♭   F C7   F
You raise me up to more than I can be.

Outro-Chorus

  A7   Dm B♭   F
 You raise me up so I can stand on mountains.

C   Dm B♭   F
You raise me up to walk on stormy seas.

C F   C   F
I am strong when I am on your shoulders.

B♭   F Csus4   Dm B♭
You raise me up to more than I can be.

N.C.   F C7   B♭ C F
You raise me up to more than I can ___ be.

The Very Thought of You

Words and Music by
Ray Noble

I don't need your pho-to - graph, _____

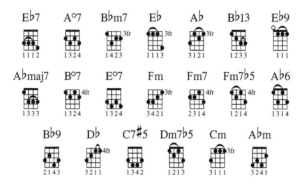

Eb7 A°7 Bbm7 Eb Ab Bb13 Eb9

Abmaj7 B°7 E°7 Fm Fm7 Fm7b5 Ab6

Bb9 Db C7#5 Dm7b5 Cm Abm

Intro |Eb7 A°7 |Bbm7 Eb |Ab | |

Verse 1
Ab   Bb13
I don't need your photograph,

Bbm7   Eb9 Abmaj7
To keep by my   bed.

Ab   B°7   Bbm7   Eb9 Ab Eb7
Your pic - ture is always in my   head.

Ab   Bb13
I don't need your portrait, dear,

Eb7   E°7 Fm
To call you to   mind,

Fm7   Fm7b5 Abmaj7 Bb13 Bbm7
For sleeping or   waking,   dear, I find…

Chorus 1

E♭9   A♭   A♭6
The very thought of you, and I for - get

       A♭   B♭m7 B°7
To do the little ordi - nary   things

   A♭   B♭9
That ev'ryone ought to do.

   D♭   B♭m7 E♭7   Fm7
I'm living in a   kind of daydream,

C7♯5 Fm   Fm7 Dm7♭5
I'm happy as a king,

B°7   Cm   A♭m E♭
And foolish tho' it may seem,

B°7 B♭m7   E♭7
To me, that's ev'ry - thing.

N.C.   A♭   A♭6
The mere i - dea of you, the longing here for you,

       A♭   B♭m7 B°7   A♭
You'll never know how slow the moments go

      B♭9
'Till I'm near to you.

   D♭   B♭m7 E♭7 Fm7
I see your face in ev'ry flower,

C7♯5 Fm   Fm7   B°7
Your eyes in stars a - bove.

N.C.   E♭7
It's just the thought of you,

A°7   B♭m7   E♭9 A♭
The very thought of you, ____ my love.

	A♭		B♭13
Verse 2	I hold you re - sponsible,		

A♭   **B♭13**
I hold you re - sponsible,

B♭m7   **E♭9 A♭maj7**
I'll take it to   law,

A♭   **B°7**   **B♭m7**   **E♭9 A♭ E♭7**
I nev - er have felt like this be - fore.

A♭   **B♭13**
I'm suing for damages,

E♭7   **E°7 Fm**
Excuses won't do,

Fm7   **Fm7♭5 A♭maj7 B♭13**   **B♭m7**
I'll only be   satis - fied with you.

Chorus 2   *Repeat Chorus 1*